Dan Jenkins

UNPLAYABLE LIES

Dan Jenkins is one of America's most acclaimed sportswriters as well as a bestselling novelist. A native Texan, he has spent a lifetime at the typewriter and computer. He might be best known for his twenty-four years of stories in *Sports Illustrated* and now *Golf Digest*. Three of his bestselling novels—*Semi-Tough*, *Dead Solid Perfect*, and *Baja Oklahoma*—were made into movies. His sportswriting has won him many awards. He was inducted into the World Golf Hall of Fame—one of only three writers to be honored thus far—and was given the PEN Lifetime Achievement Award for Literary Sports Writing. He is also the winner of the Red Smith Award, the highest honor in his profession.

UNPLAYABLE LIES

UNPLAYABLE LIES

(The Only Golf Book You'll Ever Need)

DAN JENKINS

Foreword by Sally Jenkins

ANCHOR BOOKS

A DIVISION OF PENGUIN RANDOM HOUSE LLC

NEW YORK

The Library of Congress has cataloged the Doubleday edition as follows:
Jenkins, Dan.
Unplayable lies / [by Dan Jenkins]—First Edition.
pages cm
1. Golf—Anecdotes. I. Title.
GV967.J43 2015 796.352—dc23 2014020086

Anchor Books Trade Paperback ISBN: 978-1-101-87307-6
eBook ISBN: 978-0-385-53976-0

Book design by Michael Collica

www.anchorbooks.com

For Jerry Tarde and Mike O'Malley, good bosses,
skillful editors, better friends

CONTENTS

ANOTHER SIDE OF DAD

By Sally Jenkins

My father is, sadly, a fraud. There is the public account of him, and then there is my private one, and the two don't agree at all. For instance, there is the Dan Jenkins who pretends he'd rather burn small children with cigarettes than pat them on the head, and there is the adoring, lenient father I know. There is the guy whose no-holds-barred wit can force a sharp intake of breath, and there is the husband who has been devotedly married for, at this writing, fifty-five years. There is the cavalier veranda lounger who never seemed to take a note, and there is the writer I've witnessed at home who works with unswerving concentration.

My brothers and I might be the only people, apart from my mother, who know him for the suave faker he really is. At some point your childhood becomes your own property, and you see it for what it was. When you were a child, it belonged to your parents, and they cast it in their own terms.

"You're having a happy childhood," my father told me.

"I am?"

"Yes."

"Why?"

"Because I said so."

It was a nightly ritual as we were growing up in Manhattan for him to sit with me and my brothers and share our supper before he and my mother went out for the evening. On Monday nights we ate franks and beans and they went to P.J. Clarke's. On Tuesday nights we had fish sticks and they went to Elaine's. Yet somehow my father, despite reinventing forms of journalism, writing best sellers in alarmingly casual-seeming fashion, and working on his reputation for enjoying the smartening effects of young scotches, managed to provide us with a childhood that was, in fact, happy and healthy. How did he accomplish this? One of his methods was a deceptive sobriety, another was a veiled attentiveness to his family, and yet another was a sly conscientiousness at his work.

The dinner hour was always ours. My parents would sit at the kitchen table with their three children, and their three tall glasses of milk. My father would talk to us about the world in general while he stole bites of our food, if it was brown and white.

"Daddy?" I said one evening.

"Yes?"

"I learned a joke today."

"I'll be the judge of that. Tell it."

"What's green and lives in the sea?"

"What?"

"Moby Pickle."

He began giggling helplessly, and couldn't stop for the next three minutes, while all around him, three urchins in pajamas capsized their milk with delight.

The rest of the world has its view of my father, and I have mine. It's impossible for me to read his work with professional detachment, because for every Masters or U.S. Open story, there was a family summer. The combined quality and volume of his writing on golf—and scads of other subjects—is all the more impressive to me in light of the fact that he managed to produce it while mustering private-school tuitions, attending school sports events, writing checks to orthodontists, and lifting family luggage. All of which he made seem effortless.

His fathering style was not much different from his writing style, which is to say, excellence disguised as offhandedness.

Some of the stories represent absences, but not as many as you would think. He managed to be, despite his globe-trotting, a vividly present father. He often took us with him; we scampered with impunity through pressrooms, and carried hot coffee to him on deadlines. While others might have found him acerbic, we only found him gently or hysterically funny. While his readers might be amazed to discover he had children, his children were amazed to discover he had readers.

Which is the real Dan Jenkins and which is the cunning veneer? I'll step aside and let someone else answer the question.

"Do you understand," my mother once said, "how hard your father works?"

The answer was no, at the time I didn't. It's only as an adult and a colleague that I've come to understand. Small things, details, return to me and make sense now. The curious fact that, though he was reputed to like his cocktails, I never once saw him drink at home. I recall the steady metallic sound of a typewriter as I went to sleep, and the sound of it again in the morning.

He comes from a generation of writers who adopted a demeanor of perpetual nonchalance, a cigarette smoldering at the elbow. He never talked much about writing. He never said, "Don't be a writer, you'll sentence yourself to a lifetime of excruciating self-doubt and criticism." He never said, "It's ditch-digging; it's trying to break rocks with a shovel."

He did say this: "Your dad loves his work. But I try to not let it harm the product."

As an adult, I reread the old work and look at the new, and what I see is a constant stripping away of pretense, and of the profligate excesses of feeling that surround golf, as they do other sports, to find the truth underneath. I see an unwavering effort to make sound judgments about what's humorous and what's not, what's poignant and what's not, and what's worthy and what's not.

Look at the writing in the pieces of this collection and ask yourself if it could have been as effortless to write as it is to read. Peruse the easy rhythms and the jauntiness of phrasing, and yet the unfailing truthfulness and nail-on-the-head precision in each description.

As a writer, I drew three lessons from him: the absoluteness of his concentration, the contrariness of his thinking, and the depth of his respect for good writing. All of which can only be called integrity.

"Learn your craft," he told me. "And never let a piece go until it's as good as you can make it—on deadline, of course."

So I do something others don't when it comes to my father. I take him seriously. God knows, somebody has to.

WHY COLLECT ME

I've always wanted to do something for the golfer who has everything. I thought about a suede golf cart or maybe a pair of cashmere FootJoys. Then I settled on writing this book.

It's less expensive than the green fees at most public courses. It hits hard at the truth of the sport, but hopefully with a glint. I took on the subject because I was once a scratch golfer as a collegiate competitor, and for a while afterward. But even in high school I'd learned what it was like to play the game for my own money. Plus, I've covered the sport for over sixty years now.

Half of this collection consists of original material written exclusively for this book. The other half is drawn from past magazine articles. All of it, of course, is literally throbbing with opinion. I hope the words will shine brighter than I did in the amateur tournaments I could have won but didn't, which had something to do with a higher power taking days off at my expense.

I am grateful to *Golf Digest* for allowing me to reproduce the pieces in here that have appeared in its pages over time. They have all been reworded, reshaped, updated, trimmed, lengthened, or tweaked in some way. That's the luxury of doing a collection.

Obviously I wish to thank my talented daughter for her lavish Foreword. In her own career she is a prize-winning sports columnist for the *Washington Post* and a bestselling author. She has a taste for fine red wine. To show my appreciation, I'll order her a $100 bottle the next time we dine together, but she'll probably grab the check before I can get to it. Another thing she's learned.

—D. J.

UNPLAYABLE LIES

AMERICA'S GIFT TO GOLF

I T'S EASY ENOUGH to blame America for the six-hour round, the infernal plumb-bob, the blimp-size driver, the island green, and "Get in the hole!"—son of "You da man!"—but ask yourself this: What would the game be like without the gimme, the mulligan, improving the lie, and a chili dog at the turn?

There are, of course, purists among us who eat grated persimmon for breakfast and would take us back to the square-dimple ball, the rut iron, the stymie, no sprinkler systems, and play it down everywhere, even during appendicitis attacks.

Here's the thing: America has been very good for golf, even though we may have overcooked the game, which is to say overadvanced it, and maybe overcorrected what we've overcooked.

If America hadn't become interested in the game, we might still be swinging at the ball in tweed coats, neckties, and plus-fours, and talking like Lord Crawley, the Earl of Grantham.

But do we really need a golf ball today that can puncture the side of a 68.7-ton Abrams tank when hit by an anemic fourteen-year-old girl? This is the same golf ball that can be launched from London in a high slice, correct itself over Paris, and land safely in Milan.

Which begs another question: Do we really need a 900-yard par-5 hole in our lives? The only person who might is the real estate developer who will surround it with town houses on roads named for famous courses he has never seen and therefore misspells . . . Interlacking Drive . . . Baltusroof Avenue . . . Bel-Ear Circle.

America didn't originate the gated community—I think you have to give that to Buckingham Palace—but we popularized it and contributed the windshield decal.

The golf community should be grateful for America's invention of central air-conditioning. Without it, whole sections of the world might never have been heard of, like Florida and South Carolina.

It was fine with me if a man named Stimp wanted to invent a meter. His name was actually Edward Stimpson. Lived up in Massachusetts. But I could have saved him the trouble by pointing out that putts are faster going downhill and slower going uphill, and everything in between is guesswork.

You may not know that America invented the wooden tee. Dr. William Lowell of South Orange, New Jersey, evidently a hypochondriac, was concerned about chapping his skin from forming tees out of wet sand or dirt—the preferred method dating back to Mungo Park at Musselburgh, if not before.

One day while dwelling on the dangers of sand and dirt, Dr. Lowell began whittling wooden tees out of a leg on his dining room table. He whittled them down to two inches long. Thus came the Reddy Tee, which was happily painted red by his neighbor, a fan of Cézanne, and began to be marketed in 1922.

America gave us the Tour, as you know. Once there were only the Big Ones. The U.S. Open, British Open, Western Open, North-South Open, PGA, Metropolitan Open, U.S. Amateur, and British Amateur. There were more majors than you could shake a Grand Slam at. But we added things like the Texas Open, Catalina Open, Los Angeles Open, and Miami-Biltmore Four Ball, the first corporate event.

The Four Ball was dreamed up to promote the Miami-Biltmore Hotel in Coral Gables, which may have become best known for its Al Capone Suite.

America gave us Ben Hogan, too, don't forget. Then Ben Hogan gave us practice.

What was the first corporate logo on the Tour? I know exactly what it was. I was there. The Amana hat.

We of the press in the 1960s were compelled to divide competitors on the Tour into two categories. One category consisted of Jack Nicklaus, Arnold Palmer, Gary Player, and two or three others. Everybody else was an Amana hat.

Amana was this appliance company in Newton, Iowa, a division of Maytag. Suddenly, some pros were wooed into wearing the Amana hat on the Tour for $50 a week. Julius Boros, I think, may have been the first to wear it, but he was hastily followed by Miller Barber, Dave Stockton, Lon Hinkle, Lou Graham, and several others known simply in pressrooms as "the Amana hats."

Today, as you may have observed, a Tour pro's shirt is covered with so many logos, he's in danger of being mistaken for a corridor in a shopping mall.

Research tells us that a man in Edinburgh, Scotland, named William Currie Jr. received a British patent for a metal wood back in the day of gutta-percha golf balls. He had designed a driver with a heavy brass clubhead. It never caught on. The trouble was, it worked better as a doorstop.

It's safe to say that the first workable metal wood came from the brain of Gary Adams at TaylorMade. It was a twelve-degree driver of cast stainless steel with a head about the size of a seven-wood. It made its debut at the PGA Merchandise Show in 1979.

One wonders what might have happened to this weird invention if it hadn't provided aid and comfort to Curtis Strange when he went about winning the U.S. Open in 1988 at The Country Club in Boston.

Before there was a steel clubhead there was a steel shaft. Rules makers in America approved the steel shaft in 1924. Macdonald Smith and some others of the period fiddled with it, but it didn't catch on until Billy Burke won the 1931 U.S. Open at Inverness in Toledo using steel shafts.

A man has to remind himself that Bobby Jones won all his majors and the Grand Slam swinging hickory, and without the modern sand wedge that Gene Sarazen invented in 1932.

You can thank America for the fact that you don't have so many clubs in the bag, it plants your caddie into the ground like a potato. It was our USGA that put the fourteen-club limit into effect in 1938 after a two-year argument that was called a discussion. At the time there were caddies lugging more than thirty clubs in a golfer's bag. It happens that Harry Cooper's bag contained twenty-six clubs when he won the Western Open in 1934.

We have been given the credit for numbering clubs. Prior to this, irons were known as a niblick, mashie, spade-mashie, mashie-niblick, mid-mashie-niblick, and something similar to a mid-mashie-niblick-scooper-lifter.

For better or worse, there are many other things America has contributed to the game. Just off the top of my Hogan cap, I can think of the $2 Nassau, the gangsome, cartpaths, square grooves, Softspikes, Tour caddies, Tour gurus, courtesy cars, hospitality tents, Babe and the LPGA, college golf, autograph hounds, the $500 green fee, the handicap thief, seven hundred ways to cure the slice, and the Tour Wife, which comes in two flavors today: blond and naturally blond.

Of course there will always be things to criticize about our contributions, but we'll do the criticizing, thank you. In fact, I'll start. For example, take the sports agent. Please.

IS YOUR COUNTRY CLUB
OLD MONEY OR NEW MONEY?

AS SOMEONE WHO comes from money—I was born with a silver brassie in my golf bag—it's no problem for me to tell you whether a country club is Old Money or New Money.

In fact, I'm often asked to explain the difference. The people who ask are usually public-course hackers I stop to chat with when I find them standing by the side of the road staring at the overheating radiators in their old Plymouths.

They are quick to recognize that I'm a country club guy—my golf shirt isn't faded.

One of the first things they ask is if my private club has good food. Like, you know, Fritos, Cheetos, Oreos, Moon Pies, Dr Pepper.

This is where I take time to explain that there are two kinds of country clubs. There's mine, which has age, and there is the other one, where every man plays golf in short pants, dainty anklets, and a cell phone.

The golf courses are distinctly different.

Old Money is 6,200 yards, par 76, with fourteen blind shots. The front nine is in New York, the back nine in Connecticut. It was designed by Alister Donald Blair-Tilly, who routed it on a tablecloth the night he arrived in town, which was a month after he was rescued from the *Titanic*.

New Money is 7,800 yards, par 70, and was designed by Frank (Dog) Legg, who once drove tractors for Pete Dye and Tom Fazio. It weaves around a deep, man-made rock quarry. A stretch of three holes is laid out along the shores of a newly discovered Great Lake. Other holes demand long carries over vast regions of sand where the occasional Bedouin warrior may be sighted.

Old Money's clubhouse looks like a combination of Manderley before the fire and Twelve Oaks before Ashley Wilkes went off to fight in the War of Northern Aggression.

New Money's clubhouse looks like the world's largest Taco Bell. It includes guest suites and an indoor beach volleyball court for tall young mistresses, and the Meditation Temple leads directly to the windsurfing cove and Formula One track.

Old Money's most famous hole is the short 12th, the "Swinging Casket." At twilight the member can stand on the 12th tee and gaze wistfully at the green light on the end of Daisy's dock.

New Money's favorite hole is the incredibly long 15th because it allows the member plenty of time between shots to check his text messages and make calls to say, "I'm shorting Italy."

Old Money's oldest member is still supported by the money he inherited from his great-grandfather who invented the washing machine, the electric toaster, and the ice cube.

You are not allowed to join Old Money if you've ever held a job.

New Money's oldest member invented the hedge fund.

The wife of Old Money's oldest member, Merger, is an elegant, gray-haired lady who as a young girl once sat on the lap of both Churchill and Hitler.

The wife of New Money's newest member, Georgette, is twenty-seven and currently involved in redecorating their second homes in Aspen, Zurich, London, Beverly Hills, and Prague.

One of Old Money's most popular members, Three-Hyphen Pembroke, died recently but is survived by his popular fifth wife, the sixty-one-year-old Babs, a former receptionist, who has been rebuilt to resemble a *Playboy* centerfold, and will continue to resemble a *Playboy* centerfold unless she coughs, sneezes, or smiles, in which case she will turn into Quasimodo and spend the rest of her life clinging to a gargoyle.

Most of the members at Old Money play with a set of autographed Bobby Cruickshank woods and a set of autographed Wiffy Cox irons. Their choice of a golf ball is the Spalding Kro-Flite or the bramble White Flyer.

The latest fancy of New Money members is the USS *Nimitz* driver, the Boeing 367 spoon, and a set of Exxon irons powered by compressed natural gas.

Old Money members putt with a rusted Wright & Dixon blade.

New Money members putt with what appears to be a tenor saxophone attached to the end of a drain pipe.

Old Money members never wear wristwatches—they don't have to be anywhere or do anything.

A New Money member's bulging gold Rolex lost time momentarily the other day and caused a brownout in a major American city.

Old Money members don't really follow the PGA Tour, but most of them are certain that Denny Shute could give this chap Rory McIlroy two up a side.

New Money's members don't follow the PGA Tour either, but a couple of them have heard of Rory McIlroy and would like to interest him in an investment opportunity.

Old Money will always have money.

Three members at New Money are in the process of asking the Federal Reserve for a free drop from an unplayable lie.

BEN, JACK, AND TIGER

S INCE THE COMING–AND staying—of Tiger Woods, there are friends, associates, and readers who have kept asking me to compare Tiger with Ben Hogan and Jack Nicklaus, two other guys who stacked up major championships like can goods.

I've been resisting the task, but it has occurred to me that I am surely the last remaining sportswriter who covered all three idols at their peak. If this qualifies me to take up the matter, it also qualifies me to be old.

Among the readers, there are those afflicted with the political correctness disease who think Tiger Woods should be rated the greatest of all time simply because he is a "person of color" who invaded "a white man's sport" and won a lot of tournaments. I choose to judge him on more equal footing, which is to say as a shot maker and competitor.

To begin with, there are stats to consider when appraising the three of them.

Nicklaus won his eighteen of the modern professional majors over twenty-four years. Woods won his fourteen majors over sixteen years, but it's hard to say whether he's all done or not. Hogan won his ten majors, counting the wartime U.S. Open, over eight years of competition, from '42 through '53. In the midst of that, Ben missed three years due to the war, and another year recovering from the car crash. It has to be said that Hogan's career actually started in 1940, after he'd spent five years building a game that would keep him from missing cuts and borrowing money to stay on the Tour.

In contrast to Hogan's hardships, struggles, and interruptions, Nicklaus and Woods got out of the box quickly, right out of amateur golf. Each won eight majors in his first eight years as a pro.

Throughout Nicklaus's entire career, he missed only one major because of physical problems. That was the Masters of 1983, when he withdrew after 36 with a back pain. Woods has missed six—the British Open and PGA of 2008 (knee rehab), the U.S. Open and British Open of 2011 (life rehab), and the Masters and U.S. Open in 2014 (disc surgery). Hogan missed so many opportunities to win majors due to the war, the Greyhound bus, and the aftermath, it's impossible to count them accurately. I can make a case for twenty-five at the very least.

Hogan and Nicklaus played persimmon woods, steel shafts, and the wound ball. Tiger plays metal woods, composite shafts, and a self-correcting rock for a golf ball.

Hogan also putted a "dirty" ball. Under the rules of

his day, you couldn't lift and clean on the greens. Big factor. Huge. I might add that he played on courses where the maintenance was less than exquisite.

But it's still a human that swings the club, isn't it?

Judge their "name" competitors for yourself.

Among others, Hogan competed against Sam Snead, Byron Nelson, Lloyd Mangrum, Jimmy Demaret, Cary Middlecoff, Jackie Burke, Tommy Bolt, Craig Wood, Henry Picard, Paul Runyan, Horton Smith, Bobby Locke, and Julius Boros.

Among others, Nicklaus competed against Arnold Palmer, Gary Player, Lee Trevino, Tom Watson, Johnny Miller, Billy Casper, Tom Weiskopf, Raymond Floyd, Seve Ballesteros, Greg Norman, Ben Crenshaw, and Lanny Wadkins.

Among others, Tiger competed against Phil Mickelson, Ernie Els, Payne Stewart, Sergio García, Padraig Harrington, Vijay Singh, David Duval, Retief Goosen, José María Olazábal, Jim Furyk, Davis Love III, Angel Cabrera, and Rory McIlroy.

Nicklaus won ten of his eighteen majors on three courses—Augusta National, St. Andrews, Baltusrol. Tiger won eight of his fourteen on three courses—Augusta National, St. Andrews, Medinah. Hogan won his ten majors on nine different courses. Ben's five Opens came at Ridgemoor, Riviera, Merion, Oakland Hills, and Oakmont.

Nicklaus came from behind in the last round to win eight of his eighteen majors. Hogan came from behind on the last day to win five of his ten. Tiger has yet to come from behind to win a major. In all fourteen of Tiger's victories, he was the front-runner. Is this a plus or minus where Tiger is concerned? You decide.

It's not breaking news that none of the three was Jimmy Demaret when it came to handling fandom. Or Arnold Palmer, Lee Trevino, or even Phil Mickelson. Demaret wisecracked his way through life, and won with a grin. So did Trevino. Palmer and Mickelson crashed and burned in public, but balanced it out with winning, and at various times wore their hearts outside their shirts. Fans like this.

Hogan and Nicklaus gave thoughtful and enlightening interviews about their wins and losses. They provided sensible answers to intelligent questions. Tiger's interviews—to we of the print press, anyhow—have been brief and the flip side of absorbing. Maybe he has nothing to reveal, really. Everything seems to be mechanical with him.

I never saw Ben or Jack blame anything but themselves for a loss, as bitter as it might have been. I never saw either of them sling or slam a golf club in anger and frustration. They came from an age when you held it in.

Tiger has done his share of slinging and slamming in public, but I suspect there's a reason. Winning majors came so easy for him in the beginning that when it suddenly stopped—as in the six-year lull from 2009 through 2014—something had to be blamed other than himself.

He has evidently enjoyed firing people. As I type, he's looking for his fourth swing coach, he's on his third caddie, and his second agent. Meanwhile, he's found other excuses for a dearth of majors: the knee, ankle, elbow, wrist, and disc.

I might add Tiger's six years without a major is longer than Jack or Ben ever went once they were established.

Hogan never had a guru, incidentally. Thought I'd throw this out there.

The eras bring up distinctions. Hogan came along when style and accuracy were the fashion. Fairways and greens were more important than putting. Nicklaus ushered in power golf, and was overwhelmingly long. Not just that. Jack was the first to be dominantly long AND straight. Tiger and technology have taken power to another level, and his competitors have followed. Hit it anywhere, find it, wedge it to the green, make the putt, see you on the next tee.

Nicklaus and Tiger are the two greatest putters in human history. Jack made more clutch putts that he needed, in the heat of majors, than anyone else who ever lived, until Tiger in his first ten years. Tiger sinking putts from ten to twelve feet to save pars, almost as if he took them for granted, became the game's most reliable rerun. It was golf's *I Love Lucy*. But give him credit for this. He's been the best "reader" of greens any of us has ever seen. Ninety percent of those putts went right in the throat.

Both Woods and Nicklaus were physically stronger than Hogan, and thus were longer not only off the tee but all through the bag. Strength also made them more accomplished at getting out of the rough. Not that they saw the kind of rough Ben did. On the regular Tour today the rough brings to mind chiffon.

In Hogan's day, shot making was vital. Ben never won a major with his putter. Jack, partly. Jack's long and straight tee shots, and his superb long-iron and mid-iron play entered in, *then* he sank putts.

I can think of only two majors Tiger didn't win on the greens. They would be the British Open at St. Andrews in 2000 and the British Open at Hoylake in 2006. His shot making highlighted the week.

There's no question that luck has been kinder to Tiger than it was to Hogan or Nicklaus. No player ever hit more shots into unknown terrain, for so many years, and yet was left with so many openings to the green.

To break it all down:

Driving for length with accuracy, Nicklaus.
Driving for sheer accuracy, Hogan.
Fairway woods, Hogan.
Long irons, Nicklaus.
Mid-irons, Nicklaus.
Short irons, Hogan.
Pitching wedge, Hogan.
Course management, Hogan, Nicklaus.
Bunker play, Tiger, Hogan.
Chipping, Tiger.
Rescue shots, Tiger.
Putter, Tiger.

Finally, in my infinite wisdom, I have to say that if I wanted one of the three of them to put a drive in the fairway for me, and the second shot on the green for me—*for my life*—Ben Hogan would have to hit them.

PC OVERDOSE

HOW UTTERLY TASTELESS it was for so many sportswriters to refer to Ben Hogan as Bantam Ben, the Wee Ice Mon, and The Hawk. The ugly insinuations were obvious—Ben Hogan was shorter and weighed less than some people, and though handsome, he was not as good-looking as Errol Flynn.

I can only imagine how a politically correct correspondent at the 1953 British Open at Carnoustie would have written about Hogan's masterful victory. His piece may have gone like this:

"Differently sized Ben Hogan, the vertically challenged American who fancies refrigerated items and birds of the wing, finished a golf tournament today with a 72-hole score that was in variance with the rest of the field.

"Among other golfers on the scene who chose to accept a form of gratuity for their efforts were Mr. Tony Cerda of Argentina, which is as good as any other country despite occasions of domestic turmoil, Mr. Dai Rees of Wales, whose name is as it reads and not to be mistaken for a deficiency in his spelling skills, and Mr. Peter Thomson of Australia, a fertile continent that is isolated on four sides by water, through no fault of its own.

"No golfer actually lost the event, and while this tournament was no more important than any other, the trophy was awarded to Mr. Hogan on the basis of the general opinion that fewer of his golf shots wound up in the Firth of Tay, the burns, the moist ditches, or any of the taller growth regions of the Carnoustie golf course, a public facility in the normal scheme of things."

LORD BYRON

T HAS LONG been accepted as fact and entered into worldly lore that Byron Nelson won eleven tournaments in a row and eighteen for the season in the sunny year of 1945, when the war was finally—and elatedly—coming to an end.

These two records were said to be impossible to break, ever. They would last longer than the game of golf itself, or the end of the world, whichever came first.

But here am I, all these years later, armed with nothing but a screen, a keyboard, and a mouse, to break both of those records.

The fact of the matter is, as politicians love to say, I actually credit Byron Nelson with thirteen wins in a row and twenty for the year of 1945. These two added competitions were "unofficial," but the money was spendable.

They weren't anything Byron bragged about, or wished

the record books would correct, but when I'd bring them
up with him in relaxed conversation, he'd smile knowingly.

The first one took place after the fourteenth tournament
on the '45 Tour. It was a 72-hole match between Byron Nelson and Sam Snead for the "World Championship of Golf."

The Nelson-Snead match was held over two days, May 26
and 27, when the Tour was in a two-month lull, or what
some called a hiatus if they could say it and spell it correctly.

Byron and Sam were chosen as the combatants by Fred
Corcoran, director of the PGA Tour back then, for an obvi-
ous reason. They had combined to win twelve of the fourteen
Tour events so far in '45. Eight for Nelson, four for Snead.

Earlier in the year Snead had won the L.A. Open and
at Gulfport, Pensacola, and Jacksonville. Byron had won
at Phoenix, Corpus Christi, and New Orleans before his
streak began. By the time of the match the streak was in
progress. Nelson had won five in a row—the Miami Four
Ball with Jug McSpaden, and the tournaments in Charlotte,
Greensboro, Durham, and Atlanta.

The first 36 holes were played at Fresh Meadow Country Club in Flushing, New York, on Long Island, a course
that had been host to the 1930 PGA Championship and
the 1932 U.S. Open, and was a good neighbor to Trylon
and Perisphere during the 1939 New York World's Fair.

When Nelson missed a short putt on the last green, Snead
edged him by a stroke, shooting 73-70–143 to Byron's
73-71–144.

The second 36 holes the next day were conducted at
match play at Essex County Country Club in West Orange,
New Jersey, which had nothing to recommend it other than

age, beauty, and the names A. W. Tillinghast and Donald Ross among its designers.

On a rainy day Byron whipped it around in six under par through 33 holes to beat Sam, 4 and 3. They split the prize money of ten grand in war bonds, but the press chose to add up their 72-hole scores. They conceded Byron and Sam pars on the last three holes of the match at Essex, giving Byron 69-69 and Sam 74-69. For the two days, then, they proclaimed Nelson the winner of the "World Championship" with a total of 282 to Snead's 286.

"Sam wanted to steal my five-iron," Byron once recalled. "I hit a lot of good shots with it in that match. It was my safety valve. I could hit it straight and anywhere from 130 to 180 yards. It was my favorite club. The three-iron was my other favorite. In the match I hit my three-iron 200 yards in the rain and reached the fifth hole in two, and sank a 30-foot putt for an eagle. On the next hole I hit my five-iron 170 yards to seven feet and made a birdie. That put me five up and Sam never could catch me."

The Tour resumed in the middle of June, and Byron went on with his streak by winning the Montreal Open, the Philadelphia Inquirer Invitational, the Chicago Victory Open, the PGA Championship in Dayton, Ohio, the All American Open at Tam O'Shanter in Chicago, and the Canadian Open in Toronto.

That gave him his eleventh in a row, or twelfth by my count.

The "official" streak ended in Memphis on August 19—where Nelson finished tied for fourth—but history overlooks the Spring Lake Pro-Member on the New Jersey shore that came a week before Memphis. It was a 36-hole tournament with a strong field of forty-five touring pros. Byron shot 69-71–140 to win it by one stroke over Sam Snead and Herman Barron.

Granted it was only 36 holes, and granted it was "unofficial," but the $2,200 he collected was more than the first-place money in all but five stops on the tour. When you count the "World Championship" and the Spring Lake Pro-Member to Nelson's eighteen other victories that year—he won four more times after Memphis—you come up with twenty wins.

For those who think Nelson may have taken advantage of war-weakened fields, I enjoy pointing out that Sam Snead played in twenty-six tournaments in '45, winning six of them, and Ben Hogan was released from the Army Air Corps in time to compete in seventeen tournaments, winning five.

Only eight other players won tournaments in '45. Their names deserve enshrinement: Henry Picard, Dutch Harrison, Sam Byrd, Ray Mangrum, Jimmy Hines, and three amateurs—Cary Middlecoff, Frank Stranahan, and Freddie Haas Jr., who won at Memphis. Middlecoff would become a big star as a pro, Haas would also achieve success on the Tour as a pro, and Stranahan's career was perhaps the most remarkable. Frank was not just the finest American amateur of his day—he won two British Amateurs along with seventy other titles—he won four times on the Tour while playing for fun, and twice more after turning pro.

Ironically, Byron's last victory of the year—his twentieth—

occurred in the Fort Worth Open, back in his old hometown, and on Glen Garden Country Club, the course where he and Ben Hogan had caddied in their teens.

I was in high school then and spent the week at the tournament being amazed by everything I saw, starting with Byron's fast play and crisp iron shots that enabled him to run away from a strong field of competitors that included Hogan and Snead.

I was there the day of a practice round when Jug McSpaden arrived from an exhibition in Shreveport in his single-engine airplane. He landed on the fifth fairway, a par-5, realized he'd chosen the wrong landing strip, took off, circled, and landed on the first fairway, a par-4. He taxied over to the pro shop, unloaded his clubs, and took off again to look for a local airport.

Apparently this wasn't unusual for Jug. His trademark on the circuit was playing golf in a pair of aviator glasses.

Glen Garden in that chilly middle of December looked like a parched prairie decorated with green polka dots. These were the rye greens. It was a strange layout to begin with. Par was 37-34–71, and I have yet to come across a goofier back nine in my travels. It featured back-to-back par-5s once, and back-to-back par-3s *twice*.

Byron once said, "When I was growing up, I never heard people talk about how different the layout was. Of course I didn't have much to compare it with. I do know the back nine was difficult. The 15th was a long, uphill par-3—you had to hit a wood—and the 18th was a three-iron to a small green with out-of-bounds close on the left."

When I reminded Byron of the tall electrical tower in the middle of the fairway on number 12, a par-5, he laughed and said, "Oh my, yes."

Nelson's truckload of trophies in '45 says one thing about his dominance, as does his astounding scoring average of 68.33 in thirty-two tournaments, but as stats go, I'm partial to his margins of victory.

He won by eight strokes over Sam Byrd in Greensboro, by five over Toney Penna in Durham, by nine over Byrd in Atlanta, by ten over Jug McSpaden in Montreal, by seven over McSpaden in Chicago, by eleven over Lieutenant Ben Hogan and Gene Sarazen in the Tam, by ten over Byrd in Knoxville, by seven over McSpaden in Spokane, by thirteen over McSpaden in Seattle, where he shot 259—a world record—and by eight over Jimmy Demaret at Glen Garden.

Those margins of victory bring to mind an old saying, source unknown, but it probably came from a football coach:

"It's not enough to just win, you have to let the loser know he lost."

TITANIC AND I

F EVEN HALF the stories about Titanic Thompson were true, he couldn't have lived to be eighty-two years old. Earlier in his life some gentleman in a pin-striped suit looking like Rico Bandello or Michael Corleone would have bumped him off. Big shots don't like to get robbed.

I once met Titanic. That's the big news in this effort.

I'd heard most of the stories growing up, and every article I've ever read about Titanic was written by someone who never knew him personally. But I'm not faulting them for it. A lot of people who never knew Napoleon have written about him.

Those who have rhapsodized about Titanic in print were understandably intrigued with the legend and all the outlandish gambling stories attached to him, many of them helped along by the man himself, along with the stunts and tricks he performed, or supposedly did, to fleece the unwitting in a more naive era.

The tales about him were hard to resist. He was indeed an accomplished professional gambler as well as a hustler, and those are two different things. There is solid testimony from people who did know him that he was an excellent golfer, cardplayer, pool shark, and skeet shooter. The rest is up for grabs.

I was fourteen when I first heard about Titanic. So did every kid in Texas who spent any time around golf courses. The club pros usually told the stories and pretended to know him, and some did know him, and they were prone to embellish the stories if that was needed to hold your interest.

I believed he could throw an orange or a lemon over a five-story building—I assumed he had an arm like Dizzy Dean. Of course, I later learned the orange or lemon was weighted down with lead. I never believed he could throw a brass key into a door lock from across a hotel room. That defied logic. But I did believe he could throw a roll of quarters into a snuff can from thirty feet away without missing. At a young age I was willing to believe, if not hopeful, that he had dated movie stars like Jean Harlow, Joan Blondell, and Myrna Loy.

There was a lot of romance in the stories about Alvin C. Thomas, which was his real name. Alvin Clarence Thomas of Rogers, Arkansas, by way of his birthplace, a small town in Missouri.

But I never believed he could knock a bird off a telephone wire by hitting a golf ball at it with a four-wood. I wasn't that gullible.

Then I found out how he did it if a wager was involved. Ti

would drop a ball on the ground and take out his four-wood, waggle it, and pretend to aim at the bird on the wire. When some sucker would bet him he couldn't do it, Ti would pull out a gun he carried and shoot the bird off the wire.

Years later I realized Ti could do some of the things I'd heard about, because I saw others do it. Bob Rosburg, for example, could sail fifty-two cards out of a deck, one by one, into a hat from a good distance away in a locker room.

And this day and time almost any college golfer can bounce a golf ball on the face of a sand wedge fifty times or more without missing. These days it's what a college golfer practices in the dorm instead of studying.

My first long-distance call from Titanic Thompson came in March 1970. He was then living in Grapevine, Texas, which is near Fort Worth and Dallas. I was living in Manhattan and writing for *Sports Illustrated*. The call came to my office in the Time-Life Building.

I let Titanic know how delighted I was to be speaking with a legend, after which he told me how rich we were going to be when I wrote his story for a movie and a book. All he wanted was a million dollars up front. Just a million.

As the saying goes, I may not be smart, but I'm not stupid. I was aware that I couldn't possibly be the first person Titanic—"Call me Ti"—had ever approached with the project. I must have been far down the list, or he would have sold it by this particular time in history.

I was also busy. Not only with my magazine assignments

on the road, but I was working on a novel, which happened to be *Semi-Tough*. Still, I didn't want to blow him off altogether. I told him I would ask around, talk to my agent, try to see if his story could "gain any traction in the marketplace," to use agent-speak, and we would chat again another day.

Which we did. A week later. When he called to try to stoke my interest by rolling his credits as a folklore character. I heard how he had set up the poker game at which Arnold Rothstein, a crime boss, was murdered in New York City. How he won a bundle off Howard Hughes at Lakeside Golf Club. How he took on other Hollywood folks on the golf course and "picked 'em like chickens." How he had skinned that "big fraud" John Montague at Lakeside. How he'd dated all those Myrna Loys in Hollywood in the early thirties.

That last bit of info probably didn't need questioning—it evidently wasn't that hard to do.

This requires a brief interruption, a skip forward by fifteen years. Through a mutual friend, as it happened, my wife and I were invited to have dinner with Myrna Loy—and drinks afterward in her Manhattan apartment. A swell time was had by all.

Myrna Loy was friendly and charming, and well preserved for a lady in her eighties. I had adored her on the screen as Nora Charles in all the *Thin Man* movies, and even more as Milly, the wife of Fredric March, in *The Best Years of Our Lives*. She made over eighty films.

At some point during the evening I asked her if she had ever known or gone out with a man named Titanic Thompson in her early days. I explained who he was, and that he had been well-known in certain circles.

She said, "I was making a movie every six weeks in those days. But I did have a free night now and then. What a wonderful name. Was he handsome?"

I said, "According to lore. Tall guy, elegant dresser."

"Well," she said with a sparkle, "I hope he took me to the Brown Derby."

I told Titanic I would be in Fort Worth in May for the Colonial tournament and two or three days afterward, to visit with relatives. Maybe we could get together. I wanted to meet the notorious figure in the flesh.

He was seventy-eight years old then, dividing his time between Tenison Park in Dallas and Meadowbrook in Fort Worth, two public golf courses where gentlemen of sporting blood gathered. He still fancied wagers.

I let him know I'd be staying at the Green Oaks Inn in Fort Worth. He said he'd call me there and we could arrange to meet.

The Titanic Thompson I found at Meadowbrook was a thin, white-haired man roughly six feet tall. He was wearing a long-sleeve alpaca sweater over a golf shirt, a pair of tan slacks, and a red ball cap.

First, I broke the news to him that I couldn't find any interest in a book or a movie. The book people had never heard of him, which didn't surprise me. The movie people said *Guys and Dolls* had covered the subject of gambling, and a golf movie didn't yell money at them.

I did tell him that *SI* would be interested in an article. He could collaborate with a writer on our staff, and the magazine would pay him a fee of some sort.

He said he would give it some thought.

The thing I wanted to hear about the most was his side of the legend-filled match he played against a young Byron Nelson in Fort Worth, but I led up to it with questions about other things.

I said, "You mentioned John Montague on the phone. You said 'Golf's Mystery Man' was a fraud?"

Ti said, "The biggest mystery to me was how he ever got famous. He could hit a long drive, but he couldn't break 75. Heck, if you gave me two strokes a hole, I could beat you with a baseball bat and a rake and putt with my shoe. He got all he wanted of me in one day at Lakeside. But the middle 70s was all he needed to shoot to beat those Hollywood people with low handicaps they couldn't play to. Except for Howard Hughes. Howard was a good golfer. He worked hard at the game. He took lessons. Howard wanted to win the National Amateur more than he wanted to make movies. But he was never that good."

I said, "Your reputation came in handy, didn't it?"

"It did when my name got around," he said. "I come to find out there were a lot of people who wanted to lose money to Titanic Thompson. It gave 'em a story to tell their friends. I took advantage of that."

"Golf was the game you were best at?"

"I was good at cards, too. I never cheated at cards. I played straight up. I could read cards and I could read people. I mostly played poker, but I could play any old card game. Fan

Tan, Crazy Eights, gin rummy. Gin was starting to catch on back in the thirties, but not everywhere, and not like today."

I said, "Gin was too slow, right? For a gambling man?"

"You could say that."

I wanted to hear about his name. I'd read that he adopted "Thompson" when he saw his name misprinted in a newspaper.

"Titanic Thompson does have a better ring to it than Titanic Thomas," I said as a comment, not a question.

He nodded.

As lore had it, he got the name Titanic as a young man before World War One in a pool hall in Joplin, Missouri. But I said I found it hard to buy that he got it by jumping over a pool table, or diving over a pool table, or whatever else he'd let people believe.

He said, "I did get the name in a pool game in Joplin, Missouri, before the war. A man named Snow Clark gave it to me. We were in a big game of pocket pool. Snow and me were partners against two other fellers. The stakes got pretty high. Snow saw me miss a couple of shots I should have made, and he knew it takes as much skill to miss a shot intentionally as it does to make it. He thought I'd put him in the can—that I'd bet on the other side. That's when he said, 'Boy, you're sinkin' me like the *Titanic*.' I started laughing. I knew he'd given me a great name."

"I'll take that version," I said.

In years past I'd talked to both Ben Hogan and Byron Nelson about Titanic. Each said he possessed a fine golf swing and was a hell of a player. Hogan also said, "Only a fool would play him in a game he suggested."

I brought up the match between Titanic Thompson and Byron Nelson. It wasn't covered by the press, and was never written about, but it became a part of Fort Worth golf history. They played an 18-hole match for $1,000—winner take all—in 1931 at Ridglea Golf Club on the west side of town. Ridglea was a public course then, but since 1954 it has been a country club of prominence.

One thousand was big money in those days. It would be the equivalent of $14,000 today in terms of buying power.

Ti was in town and all the public courses were gambling haunts back then. He dropped by Ridglea and let it be known that he wanted to play "the best man in town" for a thousand dollars. Word reached a member at Glen Garden Country Club, where Byron was a junior member. This was a year before Byron turned pro. He was the best amateur around the area then.

The member at Glen Garden liked games of chance, and rounded up two other investors. They backed Nelson in the match.

Byron's memory of the event:

"I never gambled at golf in my life, and I didn't want to be a part of it. I don't really remember who the backers were. A Mr. Brown was involved, but that's the only name I recall. Mr. Brown said not to worry about the money. All I had to do was play my best golf—they were taking the risk.

"Well, of course, I enjoyed competition. I wanted to play my best. About a dozen people followed us. I was nervous and bogeyed two holes and fell behind, but I played well on the back nine. We both shot 70, which was one under par, I believe. The match was a tie. We broke even."

I shared Byron's memory of the match with Titanic at Meadowbrook.

Ti said, "Byron Nelson said we tied? I know I shot a 70 and he shot 71. Ask Mr. Brown if we broke even."

Before our meeting ended, Titanic said, "I can still play a little. I'll tell you what. You let me tee it up everywhere, even in the bunkers and the rough, and I'll bet you two hundred I can shoot my age. I'll shoot a 78."

I could only smile.

"I'll bet you can too, Ti," I said.

THE NEW CLUB PRESIDENT

Dear Members:

Allow me to take this opportunity to say thanks to all of you who voted to give me the honor of leading you into an exciting new era in our country club's history, even those of you who have called me a lying, thieving, back-stabbing, lightweight phony jerk. I hear the talk.

It was a close election, but I saw the momentum swing my way when two members of my slate were released from custody before voting. I'm happy to say the charges may yet be overturned, which would be a good deal for our club as well as their families, not to mention their selves.

I refer to our two new vice presidents, Larry (Gun Crazy) Sharp and Toby (Gimme Putt) Harris. I also wish to congratulate our newly elected treasurer, S. F. (Six Fingers) Cooper, a holdover from the last regime.

There is no question we won on our slate of changes for the club. It was a forward-looking, cost-efficient platform, and overall a victory for the common man. As I argued in my campaign, country clubs need more common people in the membership, particularly those who can't afford it and have to take out bank loans.

It goes without saying there will be big changes around here, starting with the golf course.

Not just the controversial greens but the bunkers, fairways, trees, roughs, and tees. All the things the touring pros have complained about over the years.

If our annual tournament—the Deutschland Acquisition & Takeover Classic in Association with Nissan's More Than 1,200 Cargo Van Dealers—is to remain a stop on the PGA Tour, the golf course issues have to be addressed. I'm sure that's what we all want, except for the two thousand nongolfing social members who don't get parking passes, and a few sporting ladies who play tennis and mah-jongg.

First thing my regime will do is get rid of the greens. I'm sure many of you remember my campaign slogan, "Poa annua—po us!"

For years our greens have led the league in spike marks, crusty edges, and casual water.

In case you don't remember the words of Jack Nicklaus a few years back, let me remind you of what he said about our greens.

He said: "I've never been able to make a putt on a bear rug."

We're going back to our roots, is where we're going. Sand greens.

Sand greens are cheap and they're not made of sand, of course. They're made of shredded cottonseed hulls and oil. Or down on the coast where they're made of shredded seashells and buttermilk pie. I know this from personal research.

Gimme Putt Harris says he happens to have a big supply of cottonseed hulls in his backyard and he's willing to let us have it at a fair price. Meanwhile, Six Fingers Cooper says he can make a deal with a certain supermarket for all the bottles of olive oil we need, and he will take only 40 percent for himself.

I'll be bringing this up before the board.

Other improvements for the golf course, which I heartily endorsed in my campaign, will be the following:

Removal of the Greg Norman Flower Bed to the right of number 9 fairway, and also the Greg Norman Fence on number 1.

Filling in the Craig Wood Gulch on number 10.

Bringing the Arnold Palmer Tee at number 15 back onto the golf course from Mrs. Weaver's lawn across the road.

Chopping down the Gary Player Oak that hangs over the green on number 14 and disturbs the flight of everybody's second shot.

Widening the Lawson Little Shrubs on the tee box at number 6 that tend to interfere with so many drives before they get in the air.

Draining the Jug McSpaden Pond to the left of number 18 and replacing it with a structure for luxury boxes. Frankly, there's not one person in this club who knows who Jug McSpaden was, including me.

As for the food in the Triple Bogey Dining Room and

the Lateral Hazard Lounge, you can say good-bye to the ordinary BLTs, Reubens, and hamburgers. I've hired the city's most beloved chef, Neal Thrush, to dish up my personal favorites of his—the squirrel nachos, the rodent sausage, the porcupine burritos, and the Friday Night Special of fried red-lipped batfish on a bed of stewed pineapples and armadillo chunks.

For those of you who liked and were happy with Chef Ernie, I am pleased to report that he has found work at the Pancake Heaven located where Loop 820 West has a head-on with I-35 South.

Naturally I will be addressing one other matter of concern for us all. It is what we should do about the children of our young married members, the little urchins you see running loose constantly, kicking over chairs, tripping waiters, poking people in the ribs, yelling on a golfer's backswing, and peeing on the entrance hall carpet. I have some ideas that involve nets and tie-down roping.

Our future is ahead of us.
Your President,
Donny Dale Foster

MEMBER GUESTS

M Y WHOLE LIFE I've searched for the perfect member-guest partner, but always in vain. After the tournament starts I find myself trying to control a killer sigh because I'm stomping around in the rough trying to help my partner find his golf ball. This inevitably happens on a difficult hole where we badly need a par, but I'm in my pocket, and my partner suddenly introduces a swing that comes in three pieces—hula hoop, wood chop, heart attack.

Small wonder that in a lifetime of playing my heart out in member-guests I'm 0-for-Steuben. I can only dream of a partner who doesn't tell golf jokes, doesn't bully clubhouse waiters, doesn't hit on the cart girl, wears long pants, and brings a 16 he can play to without falling down.

The types of partners I've dealt with:

The Shorts and Anklets Guy

"Do you have to dress like this?" I say. "Who started this trend, a soccer team?"

"It's hot. I like to stay cool."

"Could you at least wear white socks?"

"I would look like a basketball player. Stop staring at me."

"I'm trying to envision Ben Hogan in shorts and anklets."

The New Set of Clubs Collector

He has a handy alibi. The clubs are doing it, not him.

"I usually play better than this," he says, "but I never do."

"That's actually funny."

"It's these new clubs. This hook is killing me."

"Your slice is killing me more than your hook."

"I'm sorry. I've never sliced this bad either."

"Well, I can't wait until tomorrow."

"What's tomorrow?"

"Alternate shots."

The Long-Putter Wizard

It's a tradition in my family to hate the long putter, and hating it almost as much as we hate tripe on a plate. There are many things the long putter is better suited for. Fishing. Pole vaulting. Measuring.

I say to my partner, "I don't care much for the long putter myself. It's unsightly. Especially the broomstick."

"Man, I couldn't putt without it."

"It seems to wobble in the wind."

"Yes, but it helps me on the two-footers."

"We never have a two-footer."

The Rules Official

He was put on earth to track down rules criminals. He instantly reports someone to the FBI who accidentally has more than fourteen clubs in the bag. He cautions the CIA to be on the lookout for the terrorist who gains an inch or two when marking his ball.

He said to me, "Look at that jerk who has us two down. He just moved out of a lateral hazard. That's a clear violation of 34-6, paragraph 16a, section 27."

"Was that you last week who called in the illegal drop on Tiger Woods when you were watching TV?"

"Yes. It was my moral obligation."

"They didn't penalize him, though."

"No, they didn't. He claimed an allergy did it. Watch what you're doing!"

"I'm addressing my ball."

"You're standing in the middle of a 13-2, section 3b!"

"God help us."

The Equipment Victim

He's never met an oversize composite-flex-plutonium-ceramic-fusion-wide sole-uranium driver he didn't want to take to dinner and a movie.

"Here it is, my man," he says. "You have to know the satellite coordinates before you swing this baby."

"That's the biggest one I've ever seen."

"It's the key to the vault."

"What's it called?"

"Cowboy Stadium."

The Course Dropper

He's done it all. Been everywhere more than once. He's played the Beach, the Point, the Foot, the Nole, the Hills, the Oak, the Wicker, and the Riv.

He's canned the loop at the Old. He's tested the Maid, the Shinny, and the Nash out in the Hamps.

He arrives saying, "Played the Big Track last week. Lot of Poa."

The Big Track could mean anything from Augusta National to Pine Valley.

The Val, I mean.

The Instruction Book Slave

Far be it from me to disagree with the curved left arrow pointing from my left shoe up to my right shoulder. Or the dotted line showing my clubhead leaving my shaft and flying toward Des Moines, Iowa. But this particular partner understands everything about it.

"Look at your feet," he says.

"Why?"

"You're out of position. Turn your left toe to 11:58 and keep the right foot on five after twelve."

"What time is my grip, would you say?"

"It's a little left of two fifteen."

"I have a confession to make."

"What is it?"

"I'm not a good enough golfer to read golf instruction."

FEUDS

A SERIOUS FEUD, TO my way of thinking, would be "nukeler combat toe to toe with the Rooskies," to quote Slim Pickens in *Dr. Strangelove.*

In the golfing world, however, feuds exist only in newspapers. Within the hearing of a reporter, a player can accuse another player of being a low-rent cheater after he wins a tournament by replacing his golf ball from the ankle-high rough into a decent lie without penalty, this despite the fact that there's no visible evidence that a pack of werewolves had been chewing on the ball. In retaliation, the low-rent cheater can respond in the newspapers by saying the accuser is known to mark his own golf ball on the greens with a manhole cover.

The feud will be fun for readers for a day or two before it blows away like a high slice in a Scottish gale.

To my knowledge, there has never been a feud among touring pros that involved severe fisticuffs—a man's grip could be injured, his career ended. I have only heard second-hand of an incident where an angry player shoved another player into a wall of lockers and threatened to break various limbs, but he was quickly restrained by other pros.

The incident occurred when the angry player accused the other guy of having an affair with his wife. The accused responded by saying, "I thought about it, but the line was too long."

I'm happy to report that in my dealings with touring pros, I've never taken any clavicle shots even though I've made some of them hot with the written word.

Johnny Miller didn't much like it after he shot that 63 at Oakmont to win the U.S. Open and I mentioned that the course had been softened by rain and he hadn't played "the real" Oakmont. I admit it was derelict of me not to have added that, after all, everybody played the same golf course, and it shouldn't detract from his victory.

One time while Miller was winning tournaments right and left, I wrote, "What fun is it to be Johnny Miller if the highlight of your social life is watching your kids turn over glasses of milk in a Marriott?"

He didn't mention it when we won a World Cup pro-am together in Marbella, Spain.

Johnny Miller was a tremendous player, and I'm on record as saying in print that he is by far the best golf commentator on TV, and has been for twenty years. We're friendly today when we bump into each other. I take it as an indicator that he no longer wants to bind me up in a straitjacket if there's a typewriter or a computer nearby.

Curtis Strange had issues with me, which was unfortunate, because I pulled for him. I liked his golf game and his competitive spirit. I did tease him in print for losing a Masters under the circumstances by going for 15 when he shouldn't have, and for laying up at 15 when he should have gone for it.

I also teased him for skipping British Opens when he was exempt and at the top of his game. When the USA was losing one of those Ryder Cups along the way, I wrote, "The clincher for Europe came down to a contest between Seve Ballesteros and Curtis Strange. Perfect. Here was a match between a European who wins majors and an American who skips majors."

Strange let his displeasure with me be known through a mutual friend. But years have passed and he must have decided that the things I'd written about him were true, because we had friendly drinks together at the bar in our hotel during the 2012 U.S. Open in San Francisco.

In the 1970 PGA at Southern Hills, my good friend and fellow typist Bob Drum and I spent the week rooting shamelessly for Arnold Palmer, who was playing superbly tee to green and contending for the only major title that had been escaping him. Palmer would have been the best story, and we root for good stories.

Unfortunately, the relatively unknown and more or less invisible Dave Stockton was in a "putting coma," sinking 20- and 30-foot putts for pars and bogeys all the way, and he wound up winning that PGA by two strokes over Palmer and Bob Murphy.

I couldn't resist writing a story that was more about Arnold regrettably losing than it was about Stockton winning. The tournament in boiling-hot Tulsa turned out to be the last time Palmer had a serious shot at the PGA.

Stockton wasn't happy with my story. Two weeks later at a tournament in New Jersey, he ran into Drum and said, "Is Jenkins here? I need to have some words with him."

Drum reported my absence, and said, "Whom shall I say is asking?"

I might have had a feud with Greg Norman, who was such an easy target—his meltdowns and bad luck in majors became the stuff of legend—but he was evidently too rich to care what came out of my typewriter.

When Greg went to the 72nd hole at the '86 Masters and hit a half-shank, push-fade, semislice four-iron to make a bogey and ensure that Jack Nicklaus won his storybook eighteenth major, I wrote, "Oh, well, Greg Norman has always looked like the guy you send out to kill James Bond, not Jack Nicklaus."

When he suffered the horrible luck of having Bob Tway hole out a bunker shot on the last hole to steal the '86 PGA from him at Inverness, I mentioned in print that he might have avoided the tragedy if he hadn't followed up his earlier rounds of 65, 68, and 69 with a 76.

His worst tragedy of all occurred in the '96 Masters. This was where he soared to a final-round 78 and blew a six-stroke lead, which allowed Nick Faldo to overtake him. When Faldo gave Greg a consoling hug on the last green, I reported that the sporting gesture might actually have been a Heimlich maneuver.

After one of his meltdowns, Norman was quoted as saying, "I still have confidence in myself. I could be a brain surgeon if I wanted to work at it."

To that news, I couldn't help writing, "Maybe so, but he wouldn't operate on this cowboy on Sundays."

Through all this I'm delighted to report that he never mailed a letter bomb to my home, or sent Guido to chat with me. That's what I call a true sportsman and real gentleman.

There was a moment when George Archer and his wife wanted to drive a stake through my heart. It was after George won the '69 Masters and I'd written that he still wouldn't have any charisma if he rode in a golf cart with Jill St. John. I received a letter from his wife saying, "I'll have you know my husband has more charisma than Joe Namath and Gary Cooper combined."

I thought that over and wrote her a response, but I'm happy to say I never mailed it. My note had said, "I'm inclined to agree with you about George, inasmuch as Joe Namath has a bum knee and Gary Cooper is dead."

A MOVIE GAME YOU CAN'T REFUSE

THIS COMBINES A certain knowledge of golf with a love of movies. Why would I write such a piece? I want to round up the usual suspects. So here's looking at you, kid.

Front Nine

No. 1. Do you really think you can sign Tiger Woods? How would you do that, Hughes?

"I'll make him an offer he can't refuse."

No. 2. Sorry, gentlemen, but I'm afraid you're not allowed in the clubhouse. You don't have the proper badges.

"Badges? We don't need no stinkin' badges."

No. 3. Look, I shot a 77. I've got nothing to say to you writers. I'm not going to the pressroom, so leave me alone.

"What you've got, you used to have."

No. 4. Charlie's been your caddie for years. I can't
     believe you're not taking him to the Hawaiian
     Open.
     "Charlie don't surf."
No. 5. I hate it over here. I hate the course. I hate the
     food. I hate the hotel.
     "You've come to Nottingham once too often."
No. 6. You came to Pinehurst No. 2 for the water
     hazards? There are no water hazards on Pinehurst
     No. 2.
     "I was misinformed."
No. 7. I've got Phil Mickelson, Rory McIlroy, and
     Adam Scott lined up for an exhibition in Joplin.
     What do you think?
     "Take 'em to Missouri, Matt."
No. 8. You and me are Jack Nicklaus and Tom
     Weiskopf. How bad do you want to beat these
     guys, Jack?
     *"I don't want to wipe out everyone, Tom. Just my
     enemies."*
No. 9. These South Korean girls are winning
     everything.
     *"Be advised. We got zips in the wire. For the record, it's
     my call. Put everything you've got on my pos . . . It's a lovely
     war . . . Bravo Six out."*

Back Nine
No. 10. Rhett, I'm so happy. I made two pars today.
     "Frankly, my dear, I don't give a damn."

No. 11. When did you think you had the Triple
   Crown wrapped up, Ben?
   *"Why don't you bore a hole in your head and let the sap
run out?"*

No. 12. I've won the Lancôme. Why won't you give
   me the trophy?
   *"If I live to be a hundred, I shall never understand how a
young man could come to Paris without evening clothes."*

No. 13. You've been a big winner on the Tour for ten
   years now. It might help save our tournament if
   you'll come back this spring.
   *"I stick my neck out for nobody. I'm the only cause I'm
interested in."*

No. 14. Hi, Greg. Gosh, you look thin since I saw
   you at the Masters.
   "At our last meeting, I died. It alters the appearance."

No. 15. You don't like our new mixed grill. What's
   wrong with it?
   *"Of all the gin joints in all the towns in all the world, she
walks into mine."*

No. 16. That fellow Aoki is amazing. He almost won
   the Open.
   "May August moon bring gentle sleep. Sayonara."

No. 17. Who was somebody named Cary Middlecoff
   anyway?
   "He used to be a big shot."

No. 18. You call yourself Big Bertha. You don't look
   so big to me.
   "I am big. It's the pictures that got small."

**The Films and Who Said the Lines,
in Case You Haven't Already Guessed**
 No. 1. *The Godfather* (Al Pacino)
 No. 2. *The Treasure of the Sierra Madre*
    (Alfonso Bedoya)
 No. 3. *The Barefoot Contessa* (Elizabeth Sellars)
 No. 4. *Apocalypse Now* (Robert Duvall)
 No. 5. *The Adventures of Robin Hood* (Basil Rathbone)
 No. 6. *Casablanca* (Humphrey Bogart)
 No. 7. *Red River* (John Wayne)
 No. 8. *The Godfather: Part II* (Al Pacino)
 No. 9. *Platoon* (Dale Dye)
 No. 10. *Gone with the Wind* (Clark Gable)
 No. 11. *Animal Crackers* (Groucho Marx)
 No. 12. *The Razor's Edge* (Clifton Webb)
 No. 13. *Casablanca* (Bogart)
 No. 14. *The Chalk Garden* (Deborah Kerr)
 No. 15. *Casablanca* (Bogart)
 No. 16. *Sayonara* (Marlon Brando)
 No. 17. *The Roaring Twenties* (Gladys George)
 No. 18. *Sunset Boulevard* (Gloria Swanson)

THEY DID IT FOR THE ALAMO

THE STUNNING VICTORY by the USA in the 1999 Ryder Cup at Brookline remains the greatest comeback in the history of golf, or apparel.

For the inside scoop on how the Americans prepared for the incredible win, it happens that I had bugged the team's private dining room on that crucial Saturday night as they talked of rallying themselves from eight points down after two days of losing four-balls and foursomes—and there were only twelve singles matches left.

On this tape you hear the words of everyone who had a part in the riveting comeback.

Dining sounds in background. Forks hitting plates, glasses tinkling.

CAPTAIN BEN CRENSHAW: I want all of you to know I feel good about tomorrow. I'm a great believer in fate. Fate's gonna take care of us.

MALE VOICE: What can fate do about our shirts?

BEN CRENSHAW: What do you mean?

MALE VOICE: We've been wearing olive drab, black, brown, and gray all week. I've taken a sneak look at our uniforms for tomorrow. Our shirts look maroon and they got splotches all over them.

JUSTIN LEONARD: I think that must be the color Francis Wee-may wore when he beat Vardon and Ray here.

PAYNE STEWART: I think it's Francis Cue-may, Justin.

BEN CRENSHAW: It's Francis Wee-met. And he upset Vardon and Ray right here at The Country Club, like we're gonna do tomorrow.

DAVID DUVAL: Who are Vardon and Ray?

JULIE CRENSHAW: Since the subject of our uniforms has come up, I would like for everybody to know I had only $275,000 to work with.

BEN CRENSHAW: I know some of you are gonna hear that our shirts look like a spaghetti Bolognese, but I think they're neat. Those splotches are pictures of a lot of our past Ryder Cup teams—and it doesn't bother me too much as a Longhorn that they're Aggie maroon. Shirts don't swing the club.

FEMALE VOICE: I can't believe y'all are sitting here talking about shirts. You're getting your brains beat out by a bunch of European waiters and dishwashers. I mean, who *are* these people?

JEFF MAGGERT: Nobody, man. We're still the twelve greatest players in the world, even when we lose.

TOM LEHMAN: We need to get the crowd into it early.

HAL SUTTON: Fist pumps help.

TIGER WOODS: I don't know. I did a fist pump Friday and almost threw my shoulder out. Nobody cared but Michael Jordan. I guess it would have helped more if Lehman and me hadn't been two down to the dishwashers.

PHIL MICKELSON: It's not easy to play your best when the crowd's yelling, "Go, Sergio" ... and ... "How do you like *this* exhibition, rich guy?"

AMY MICKELSON: That was so ugly. I can't believe anybody would say something like that to Phil.

DAVID DUVAL: Who's Phil?

BEN CRENSHAW: Sergio's a great kid. Close to the best in the world, too.

TIGER WOODS: I wouldn't go that far.

JULIE CRENSHAW: I don't see how they can be so far ahead of us. We have way more Bushes here than they do. We have President Bush, First Lady Barbara Bush, Governor George W. Bush, and Governor Bush from some other state.

ROBIN LOVE: People, may I have your attention? I want to read you something inspiring. It comes from Harvey Penick. He says in his little red book, "Take ... dead ... aim."

Long pause.

STEVE PATE: That's it?

ROBIN LOVE: I think it's very inspiring.

STEVE PATE: Take dead aim at *what*?

DAVID DUVAL: Who's Harvey Penick?

Applause as Texas governor George W. Bush makes a surprise entrance.

GOV. BUSH: You fellows aren't in as much trouble as the heroes of the Alamo, but maybe you can take heart from what Colonel William Travis, the brave commander, said to his troops in the middle of that gallant battle.

BEN CRENSHAW: I invited Governor Bush to speak to you and lift your morale.

GOV. BUSH: If I may proudly quote the colonel: "I am besieged with thousands of troops under General Santa Anna. We have sustained constant bombardment and cannonade. The enemy has demanded we surrender and lay down our maroon shirts with splotches, otherwise we will be put to the sword or left with Mark O'Meara as our only hope. I have answered with cannon shot, and our black, brown, and gray shirts of the first two days still wave proudly over the wall. We are determined to sustain ourselves as long as possible or die like brave men who never got to wear the red, white, and blue."

BEN CRENSHAW: Thank you, Governor. Now before we go to war tomorrow, I want to say this one more time. I did *not* have uniform discussions with that woman.

THE SPEECH

TRANSCRIPT OF CAPTAIN Hal Sutton's speech to the press after the USA suffered its worst Ryder Cup loss in history to Europe in 2004:

Man, I can't tell you how bad I wanted our little dogies to beat them European polecats. Why tarnation, we're the greatest golfers in the world, us being from the United States of Amurka and most of Florida, while they're from England and London and Spain and a lot of other places outside Russia. They probably had a Norwegian stuck off somewhere in case of an emergency. Several of my rawhides had never been around Europeans. To calm 'em down, I said, "You don't need to have been to Europe to see what they're like. Just spend two or three days up in New York City—you'll be lookin' right at 'em."

That got kind of a laugh.

As our Ryder Cup captain this time at Oakland Hills in Dee-troit, I wanted to jump on the Europes real quick and stuff 'em in our saddlebags. That's why I went out early with Trigger Woods and Thrill Mickelson, my two top ranch hands. They're stronger than new rope.

How was I to know they wouldn't hardly speak to one another, and just in general play like hospital food?

Somebody said Woods and Mickelson don't like each other, and that's why they didn't have no chemistry on the golf course. I said, "Well, son, I been around this game longer than most rivers have been wet, and I ain't never yet seen a test tube or a Bunsen burner make a birdie."

People asked me why Tiger Woods snubbed the press. Why he wouldn't go to the pressroom after he lost three out of four matches the first two days. I said, "Well, I ain't Socrates or one of them other teachers at Harvard, but I know this much: you can't tell a cattleman what to do if he's got a bigger spread than you do."

Phil Mickelson made me proud, I have to say. He went in the pressroom and took his medicine. He tore his heart out of his chest and throwed it on the floor. I was honored to pick it up and give it back to him.

I congratulated my opposing captain, Bernhard Landers, even though he's from Germany. And I congratulated Sergio García. Sergio went undefeated for the week, scoring four and a half points. Funny thing about Sergio. He does good in these Ryder Cups, but when he comes over and tries to play on our Tour, he can't chew loose eggs.

I also shook the hand of Colin Montgomers for scoring their winning point on Sunday. It must have felt awful good, seeing as how his wife went O. B. on him this year. I could identify with that. I've had wives go O. B. and others that DQ'd on me. Ever how many it's been.

Somebody said that when we got whipped 18½ to 9½ it was one of the few times Amurka has been held to single digits. Well, I say you can't call it single digits if you count that doodad hangin' on the 9.

We're lickin' our wounds, but I still say we're the greatest golfers in the world, and I wouldn't take nothin' for being associated with this bunch of ringtailed tooters, even though they turned out to be all hat and no cattle.

THEY SAID IT

I N THIS JOB there are quotes that rarely make print because in the moment of typing they didn't fit the theme of the piece. But they never go away. They curl up in a corner of the brain and mind their own business, like an off-brand vegetable you quietly nudge to the side of the plate.

Here's a batch I've saved up that warrant more exposure:

Gene Sarazen, during an interview when we were sitting on the porch at the Augusta National:
"We owe a greater debt to Walter Hagen than we do to anything else that's happened in this game. Walter took the club pro out of the kitchen and the repair shop, and put us on the map."

Sam Snead mulling over his tragic 8 on the last hole of the '39 U.S. Open at Spring Mill:

"I could have parred the dang hole with three seven-irons if somebody had told me what I needed. If I'd won that Open, I'd have probably won six more."

Ben Hogan on the subject of Snead:
   "If I could caddie for Sam, he'd never lose a golf tournament."

Jackie Burke, being instructive:
   "Never hit a hook. You can't talk to a hook."

Byron Nelson in a telecast when asked by Chris
      Schenkel how he could tell that Raymond
      Floyd hit a four-iron from that far away in the
      fairway:
   "Well, Chris, I've always been able to see very well as far as my eyes are concerned."

Arnold Palmer to the writer Bob Drum, who
      had cowritten Arnold's first book, *Hit It Hard*,
      when Drum asked him for a golf tip months
      later:
   "Didn't you read my book?"

Peter Jacobsen during the 1988 U.S. Open at The
      Country Club in Brookline, Massachusetts:
   "The Country Club. Couldn't anybody think of a name for this place?"

Jay Hebert in a moment when he became a good
    fortune-teller. This was in 1957 and I had asked
    him what in his estimation were the main attri-
    butes that were turning Ken Venturi into the next
    great player.
    "Ken Venturi's not the next great player. Arnold
Palmer is."

Bob Rosburg at a Tour stop when he was still a
    competitor:
    "I saw the pairing of Marty Furgol, Jerry Barber,
and Doug Ford today. They were playing three
onesomes."

Fred Corcoran, while running the 1973 World Cup in
    Marbella, Spain, when I asked him who a certain
    busybody French official was:
    "Just another guy in a five-and-a-half shoe."

Jack Lemmon on being rejected for membership
    at Bel-Air Country Club because his wife was
    Jewish.
    "I said all I want to do is play golf—I'll eat in
the car."

Don January on his friend Miller Barber half bowing
    and saying "How are YOU?" to foreign officials
    when competing overseas:
    "That's his French."

Tom Weiskopf on the British Open before he won
    one:
    "The British Open's not a golf tournament. It's camp-
ing out."

Lee Trevino on Jack Nicklaus:
    "Jack Nicklaus is the greatest player who ever lived,
or ever will live. But he can't chip. God doesn't give you
everything."

Ed Sneed, on a practice range in Florida when asked
    how his game was shaping up:
    "My wedges aren't nestling."

Ken Venturi, telling the first golf joke after the moon
    landing:
    "Hear what Neil Armstrong really said when
he stepped on the moon? That damn Trent
Jones."

Jack Nicklaus, after making a quadruple-bogey 7 at
    the 12th hole and then making four straight bird-
    ies in the 1991 Masters:
    "You have to put such things out of your mind."

Tom Place, when he was in charge of the press,
    noticing that the media tent at the 1974 PGA at
    Tanglewood was built on a slope:
    "This is the first time you'll have to play a downhill
break to get to your typewriter."

Hord Hardin, when he was Masters chairman,
  repeating what he said to Gene Sarazen after
  Gene told Hord he no longer wanted to hit a
  ceremonial drive—he was starting to feel like an
  exhibit in the museum:
  "Gene, the people don't want to see you play golf, they
just want to see if you're still alive."

Kathy Whitworth on winning more tournaments
  than any other lady:
  "I wasn't Babe or Mickey, but I could get it in the hole
around the greens."

Jimmy Demaret on the subject of certain pros trying to
  combine playing the Tour with announcing on TV:
  "They need to come down off the tower. That tower
restricts your backswing."

George Low, the world's greatest putter, on making a
  living at it.
  "I never bet Ky Laffoon on the putting green. He was
part Indian. He could see in the dark."

Hale Irwin whiffed a 2-inch putt on the last green in
  the third round of the '83 British Open at Birkdale.
  It would have ultimately given him a tie with Tom
  Watson. Now while watching Watson needing
  only an easy two putts to win on the 72nd green,
  Hale said:
  "If he doesn't two-putt this, I'll kill him."

Dave Marr, upon hearing that one of Arnold Palmer's good friends, a dentist, carried a ball marker he'd made out of the gold from Arnold's teeth:

"We're just happy he's not a proctologist."

THIS OTHER GUY SAID IT

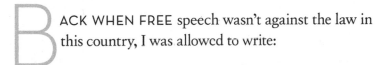ACK WHEN FREE speech wasn't against the law in this country, I was allowed to write:

A Round of Golf

A round of golf should never take more than three hours. Anything longer is not a round of golf, it's life in Albania.

Big Moment in Journalism

So this guy came up to me in a hotel bar one time. He was wearing the blazer of a tournament sponsor. He said, "Aren't you Dan Jenkins?" I said I was guilty. He said, "I've read some of your stuff. Man, you've got a problem."

I said, "No, you've got the problem. I've got the typewriter."

Masters Spectators

It was more fun observing badge wearers in the old days—before every fan was checked out at the gate by the FBI, the

CIA, and Delta Force. On the exclusive clubhouse veranda you could always find more than one guy in a baseball cap and a Georgia Bulldogs T-shirt wearing a badge that said:

> Clubhouse
> Schuyler Bevin Pendleton III
> Old Saybrook, Connecticut

"Call Me Sergio"
That's what Sergio García told the press in an interview before the '99 British Open at Carnoustie. Then he shot 89-83, missed the cut, fell tearfully into his mother's arms, and earned a new name: "Call Me a Cab."

The Comeback
Ian Baker-Finch was a surprise winner of the 1991 British Open at Royal Birkdale, then disappeared. When he attempted a comeback at Troon in '97 he appeared to be a bit wild off the tee. His round consisted of 92 strokes, 4 dead, 55 injured, 67 missing.

The LPGA
There is serious talent out there, but they can use some advice in public relations. Why? Because a competitor's idea of a good quote for the press is, "I thought it was a five-iron, but it was a six."

Name Change
When Deane Beman was the commissioner of the PGA Tour, he sat still one day and let the TPC, the "fifth major,"

become the Players Championship. It was about time. TPC sounded like something kids sniff.

The Good Old Days
The opening ceremony at the Ryder Cup used to include the anthems of each European team member. You could always tell Spain's. It was the one that never ended.

Rally Killers
The USGA used to provide the best at U.S. Opens. We looked forward to the person conducting interviews every year. For example, if a tournament leader in the media center might reveal, "I'm getting divorced and marrying a set of Siamese twins and moving to Calcutta," the rally killer was sure to say, "Fine. But let's get back to the eight-iron shot at 16."

Hoylake, Lytham, Birkdale, Sandwich
If you ever see people swimming in the freezing water at one of these seaside towns in England that hosts the British Open, you know they must have been in a shipwreck.

St. Andrews, Troon, Turnberry, Muirfield, Carnoustie
Memo to Americans going to Scotland: Never order the haggis.

My Best Prediction
I'm on record for writing that only two things could stop Tiger Woods. Injury or a bad marriage.

A Fond Farewell

Much of the conversation on the Augusta National veranda
centered on the fact that this was Pat Summerall's last Masters for CBS. Some spoke of it with such gloom you felt Pat
would be taking one of the huge veranda trees with him to
the Fox network. The subject got so out of control, one writer
hysterically compared Summerall to Pavarotti, and went on
to suggest that Pat's "arias" were irreplaceable. That statement prompted many of us to dash out and buy Pavarotti's
famous recording of "Let's Go to Sixteen."

The Print Press

For the 1993 U.S. Open at Baltusrol, we stayed in a USGA-
arranged hotel near the Newark airport. It was the one with
the tall wire fence around it with barbed wire on top. More
than one car handed over to valet parking was never seen
again.

That was also the Open of "Bus 178." The trip from the
hotel to Baltusrol normally took twenty minutes, but one
morning it took three hours and thirty minutes due to a
moron at the wheel. I was on that bus. So was my colleague
Bob Verdi, who at one point during the journey came up the
aisle saying, "Excuse me, I have to go shave again."

At the 2001 PGA in Atlanta we stayed in a PGA-arranged
hotel that was scheduled to be demolished the day after the
tournament. We went a week without hot water, room service, TV, or air-conditioning. Grand Slam.

Of course, it's an established fact that nobody has any
sympathy for sportswriters. We get in free. All we need is a
bed, a shower, and a phone to call Domino's Pizza.

A Goofy Open
In a Calcutta pool at Oakland Hills, the winner Steve Jones would have gone for a dollar in a field with Alex Cejka and Javier Sanchez. Or as Ken Burger, a writer friend then working in Charleston, said of Jones's victory, "This beats the odds on Lou Gehrig dying of Lou Gehrig's disease."

Another Goofy Open
If Andy North and Lee Janzen can each win two U.S. Opens, so can Retief Goosen. That's about all Shinnecock Hills proved in 2004.

An Award by Any Other Name
Does anyone else find it amusing that the Ben Hogan Award for the Top Male College Golfer of the Year is named for a man who never finished high school?

Progress
If Arnold Palmer once took the game to the people, can it now be said that John Daly has taken it to the trailer camps?

The Tiger Slam
When Tiger Woods won the 2001 Masters after winning the last three majors of 2000, writers wrenched muscles trying to figure out what to call it. Bobby Jones had achieved the Impregnable Quadrilateral in 1930, but what was this? It had occurred over two calendar years, but it was still a slam of some kind—wasn't it?

Efforts ranged from the Phi Granda Slamma to Four for the Road to the Fiscal Slam to the Bum Slam to the Thai

Slamma Granda to the Mulligan Slam to the Woods Wins Quartet. None of them stuck.

Everybody's Top Tweet

When Europe whipped the United States for the eighth time out of the past ten competitions, I couldn't stop myself from tweeting:

This will be quite the celebration for the Europeans when they all get back home to Florida.

Another Voice Heard From

When a young Tour player named David Ogrin disagreed with my prose once too often, he wrote my editor to complain about it, describing me as "a hostile voice from a preceding generation."

I was swollen with pride.

ATTACK OF THE SNIPPETS

L IKE ANY PROWLER through golf history, I've come across snippets and stats that lodged in the brain and found a home. Mainly they come in handy for boring dinner companions. For instance, I've been known to interrupt the entrée by leaning into the table and saying, "You probably don't know this, but Hale Irwin won a Triple Crown. He won his first U.S. Open at Winged Foot wearing eyeglasses, his second Open at Inverness with braces on his teeth, and his third Open at Medinah in contacts."

Other snippets of more than casual interest—to me at least:

Arnold Palmer never won another major after he stopped smoking.

Ben Hogan's first name was William. Billy Hogan could never have won a Doral, much less a major. Welterweight Willie Hogan? Hardly.

John was Byron Nelson's first name. John Nelson for the House of Representatives, not golf.

Bobby Jones's middle name was Tyre. Could Tyre Jones have won a Grand Slam? Maybe in NASCAR.

Only two players have won the same major six times. Jack Nicklaus in the Masters, Harry Vardon in the British Open.

Walter Hagen is the only player to win the same major four years in a row. The PGA from 1924 through 1927.

Only three players have won the same major three years in a row. Ben Hogan in the U.S. Opens of '48, '50, '51. He was forced to miss '49—the car crash—remember? Willie Anderson in the U.S. Opens of 1903, 1904, 1905. Peter Thomson in the British Opens of '54, '55, '56. Ralph Guldahl in the Western Opens of '36, '37, '38.

Julius Boros is still the oldest player to win a major. He was forty-eight in the '68 PGA at Pecan Valley in San Antonio.

The PGA Championship has been played in nine different months. All but January, March, and April. Yes, even twice in December, once in February.

Only five amateurs have won a U.S. Open—Francis Ouimet, Jerry Travers, Chick Evans, Bobby Jones, and Johnny Goodman.

Only five players have won all four modern majors— Gene Sarazen, Ben Hogan, Jack Nicklaus, Gary Player, and Tiger Woods. But Jack did it four times.

Lawson Little won the U.S. Amateur and British Amateur in 1934, and did it again in 1935. The press never came up with anything better to call it than the "Double Little Slam."

When Lawson Little turned pro he became part of a

Spalding exhibition stable that included Harry Cooper, Horton Smith, and Jimmy Thomson. They traveled together by train and did clinics and staged matches with one another before a Tour event would get under way. Jimmy Demaret named them "The Trained Seals."

Greatest feat by a geezer: Tom Watson, age fifty-nine, missed a putt on the seventy-second green, then lost the four-hole playoff for the 2009 British Open at Turnberry to Stewart Cink.

Second greatest feat by a geezer: Sam Snead at the age of sixty-two tied for third at the 1974 PGA at Tanglewood, only three back of the winner, Lee Trevino.

Third greatest feat by a geezer: Sam Snead again. At sixty years of age he tied for fourth in the 1972 PGA at Oakland Hills, which was won by Gary Player.

Fourth greatest feat by a geezer: Ben Hogan was fifty-five when he finished third in the 1967 Colonial National Invitation, three back of winner Dave Stockton.

Fifth-greatest feat by a geezer: Harry Vardon was fifty when he tied for second in the 1920 U.S. Open at Inverness, one stroke behind the winner, Ted Ray.

Sam Snead never won a U.S. Open. Arnold Palmer and Tom Watson never won a PGA. Byron Nelson never won a British Open. Lee Trevino never won a Masters. How thoughtless of them.

Craig Wood was the first player to become a runner-up in all four majors. He lost the '33 British Open to Denny Shute in a playoff, lost the '34 PGA final to Paul Runyan, lost the '35 Masters to Gene Sarazen in a playoff, and lost the '39 U.S. Open to Byron Nelson in a playoff.

Only four other players have been a runner-up in all four majors: Jack Nicklaus, Arnold Palmer, Tom Watson, and Greg Norman. Jack, incidentally, did it four times. Phil Mickelson would be in there except for the Masters. He's never been a runner-up there. He just has five thirds.

Sam Byrd is the only athlete to play in a World Series baseball game and the Masters golf tournament. He spent six seasons with the New York Yankees and two with the Cincinnati Reds in the early thirties. He took up golf in '37 and won six times on the Tour, finished third in the '41 Masters, and was runner-up to Byron Nelson in the '45 PGA Championship.

Most difficult major championship venue to reach from a civilized American city: Whistling Straits in Wisconsin on the shores of Lake Michigan if you start from Milwaukee. Runner-up: the Ocean course on Kiawah Island, South Carolina, if you start from Charleston. Nothing else is remotely in contention.

Horton Smith, "the Joplin Ghost," won the Masters on two different courses. His first win was in 1934, when the back nine was the front nine. His second win came in 1936 after the nines had been reversed. He also won the North and South Open on two different courses. Pinehurst No. 2 had sand greens when he won it in '29 and Bermuda when he won it again in '37.

Golf's ten oldest tournaments are (and were): British Open (1860), British Amateur (1885), U.S. Open (1895), U.S. Amateur (1895), Western Open (1899), North and South Open (1902), *News of the World* Match Play (1903),

Canadian Open (1904), Metropolitan Open (1905), French Open (1906), PGA Championship (1916).

Favorite AP description of touring pros: "Dr. Gil Morgan, the non-practicing optometrist" . . . "Methodical Dr. Cary Middlecoff, the former dentist" . . . "Colorful Jimmy Demaret, golf's goodwill ambassador" . . . "Purple Heart veteran Lloyd Mangrum, the mustached magician of the fairways . . ."

In case you missed the item, when Rory McIlroy won both the British Open and PGA in 2014, he became only the fourth player to have won four pro majors by the age of twenty-five. Nice company he joined: Bobby Jones, Jack Nicklaus, Tiger Woods.

And this just in. Gene Sarazen was born Eugenio Saraceni. If he hadn't changed his name and taken up golf, he could have been mayor of New York City.

SENIOR GOLF

NO ONE WAS more stunned than I when news arrived that the PGA Senior Tour—excuse me, the Champions Tour—was going to make a vigorous stab at improving its public relations. It announced that it would allow, if not encourage, fans to engage in conversations and even ask questions of the competitors during a tournament round.

I seriously doubt that the players were consulted on this decision. The last time I was around them, they seemed to be as grumpy today as they were on the regular Tour.

Upon being distracted in the midst of a round, I can hear them dredging up one of their familiar complaints: "This is my office. Would I bust into your place of business without an appointment?"

If I ever lost my way and wandered onto their Tour again, I would ask these questions:

Which hip is it you're going to have done?
Didn't you score better when you smoked?
What's the longest you've ever kept a courtesy car?
Is that a nine-wood?
Are those deck shoes better for your gout?
Do you guys ever play courses longer than 6,200 yards?
Doesn't it hurt to swing like that?
Didn't your first wife throw your clothes out in the
    front yard?
Does your caddie keep enough Demerol in the bag?
Isn't it lonely out on the course?
Do you have a favorite Motel 6 on the Tour?
How much do you miss the free shirts, slacks, and
    sweaters?
What's it like in Snoqualmie, Washington, these days?
Whataburger or Jack in the Box?
How did you vote on wives inside the ropes?
I guess you leave off the stool softeners during a tour-
    nament, right?
Can you name another profession where you get a
    mulligan in life?
Do you carry extra batteries for the hearing aids?
I said, "DO YOU CARRY EXTRA BATTERIES
    FOR THE HEARING AIDS?"

Look, I know what it's like to be a senior. I'm still looking for the glass of iced tea I put down somewhere when the
doorbell rang last week.

And I guess I'd still be playing golf too if I could hit it from
the front porch past the sidewalk.

TRUE FICTION

ASK ME IF I've read one of those advice columns for teen girls in the newspapers, and I'll say, "Yeah, all the time, don't I look like I have an eating disorder? Don't I look like I need help finding the mall?" Hey—it's the millennium, and I think I've pretty much figured out how to deal with my iPhone.

Still, I wasn't about to pass up a chance to cover the Emily Turner Clambake at Rancho Trusto Fundo. It was the year's first major. Emily Turner, in case you don't know, is the woman who influences the lives of so many young girls in her syndicated column, "Babbling with Emily," and on her popular daytime TV show by the same name.

For instance, if a teen babe wants to know where to buy a pair of cheap chandelier earrings, she asks Emily. If a teen babe wants to know what Lady Gaga is really like, she asks Emily. Emily knows a lot of things about life, and over the past five years she's become a hurricane force in golf.

Rancho Trusto Fundo Country Club is carved out of the melted cheese, chili con carne, and chopped taco salad of a California area only an hour from La Jolla. It's the most difficult course that Jack Nicklaus, Tom Fazio, Pete Dye, and Ben Crenshaw ever collaborated on—even tougher than Piranha Nibbles, the layout they designed along the banks of the Amazon in a part of the Brazilian jungle that can be reached only by paddleboat.

Rancho Trusto Fundo weaves through a residential area where all the homes look like two Merions and three Winged Foots attached to the Baltusrol clubhouse. You could say the hills are alive with the sound of money, not to write a Broadway musical about it.

But it's sort of a fun place, I learned. When you're not playing golf, you can relax on the clubhouse terrace and watch the daily swarms of illegal immigrants come romping happily over the terrain in their quaint regional costumes.

I found Emily Turner to be a trim, bouncy little thing. She was rather attractive for someone between the ages of sixty-five and eighty-four, depending on which side of her recent facelift you were standing on. I tracked her down in a clubhouse bar when I arrived. The Shank-Ri-La Lounge.

I explained how I was looking forward to covering women's golf. All my life I'd covered the PGA Tour for *Rampant Instruction*, the largest-selling golf monthly. But I'd finally grown tired of trying to get quotes out of a billionaire college dropout who didn't know how to do anything but hit a golf ball and would be hard-pressed to find another line of work outside a Walgreens.

The last straw was on the Masters veranda a year ago when I wanted to interview Sluggo Simpson, but he said he couldn't speak to me without obtaining the approval of his agent, Kaiser Wilhelm.

That was when I said before walking away, "Tell you what. Instead of trying to contact your agent, I think I'll call a brain surgeon and see if I can have your name cut out of my mind."

I told Emily I was now writing for *Divots Galore*, the golf weekly that kept fans informed about golf throughout the world. The magazine was devoted to golf literature and presenting full-page ads of chicks and guys in thong underwear.

I asked Emily how she happened to become interested in golf in the first place.

She said, "You could say it started with Bing Crosby. He was such a wonderful person, and I loved his songs. Straight down the middle . . . ba ba ba boom. And Dinah was an influence. My friend Dinah Shore. Hidy, y'all."

"I see," I said.

"All seven of my husbands played golf. They played in the old Crosby every year. I would go with them. Phil Harris was such fun."

"The Monterey Peninsula is scenic," I said.

"It's a charming part of the state, particularly if you like abalone."

"Did you say all seven of your husbands played golf?"

"Every waking moment, sweetie."

Emily revealed that her seventh and last husband, Flash Vandertip, was the person who encouraged her to start the women's Clambake. The tournament ran smoothly at first, but two years ago it broke up her marriage. Flash Vandertip fell in love with the winner, the sixteen-year-old Katie Koonce. Their age difference presented a problem, but his large private jet that was equipped with two bedrooms, a fireplace, and a putting green had won her over. They traveled to tournaments, or otherwise simply flew around the world and looked down at things. But Flash suddenly died last February. His heart exploded on the plane while Katie was looking at a golf instruction video and he was thumbing through a *Victoria's Secret* catalog.

Emily finished her highball and said I had to excuse her—she had a column to dash off about a horribly overweight actress who never—ever—should have agreed to appear on *Dancing with the Stars*.

I spent the rest of Wednesday looking over the golf course, all 7,800 yards of it from the back tees, or what the members call the "portfolios," and then studying up on women's golf. The Clambake program told me all I needed to know about the contestants.

The LPGA's five majors last year were all won by lurkers. Lang Lo Li captured the Clambake, Li Lang Lo took the iPod Invitational, Mi See Too ran away with the Mall Rat Classic, Oh No Ho scooped the Whataburger LPGA, and the Frosted Flakes U.S. Women's Open went to Su Yu Fong.

This year's Clambake was drawing its strongest field to date. The sixty invited players, who would do battle over 36 holes of stroke play, came from thirty-two states and six different countries, and among them had won 1,569 tournaments, counting junior amateurs.

Another statistical breakdown showed that sixteen of them were named Paula, sixteen were named Michelle, six were named Lolita, and the other twenty-two were South Korean.

When I looked around the pressroom I was surprised to find so many other writers on hand. Men and women were there to report for *Teen Vogue*, *Chick*, *Parent Zap*, *Hottie*, *Back Talk*, *Me!*, and *Greed*. Then there was the lady from the *New York Times* in a blue blazer, white blouse, khaki skirt, and Boston Red Sox cap. Not to overlook the AP guy in his cargo shorts, sneakers, and sombrero, with his iPad, chair seat, binoculars, and backpack of fresh fruit and bottles of natural spring water.

Emily arranged for a cart in the pro shop that allowed me to drive around as I watched the ponytails challenge Rancho Trusto Fundo in the first round of the Clambake. The lady from the *Times* and the AP guy were offered carts but refused the courtesy. They said golf carts didn't exist in O. B. Keeler's day when he covered Alexa Stirling, so why should they use one?

I stuck with the feature twosome, going the full 18 with Paula Jean Wagner and Michelle Janine Fox. Paula Jean, the fetching sixteen-year-old phenom, shot a four-under 68. Michelle Janine Fox, the other fetching sixteen-year-old phenom, finished two strokes back with a 70.

Paula Jean Wagner's success since the age of six had turned her mother into a terrified mute and her father into a limping invalid from holding down five jobs at once to pay for his daughter's private schools and golf academies. Michelle Janine Fox had been a childhood dynamo herself, winning more than two hundred tournaments since the age of seven. She had been found innocent of beating her mother to death with the 120-pound scrapbook her mother kept on Michelle Janine's career. A bushy-haired stranger uncovered by IMG, her agency, was eventually charged with the crime.

Michelle came to the pressroom first. Emily Turner pushed a slender, frightened-looking girl with a stutter out of the way and conducted the interview herself. The slender, frightened-looking girl with a stutter, I learned, was Becky Tracy, Emily's PR officer, travel agent, and shopper.

Emily said, "Michelle, would you care to make a general statement about your round before we go through your card?"

"No," Michelle Janine said.

"No? No, what?" said Emily.

"I hate my round."

Michelle Janine stared off into the distance, tight-lipped.

"But you shot a wonderful 70," Emily said, smiling.

"I took a dirt nap," Michelle Janine said.

"You took a 'dirt nap'? What in the world is that?"

"It's a dirt nap; what do you think it is?"

Emily said, "You're saying 'dirt nap,' like somebody would lie down in the dirt and go to sleep?"

Michelle Janine said, "I played like a dead man, dumbo."

Emily started to say something, but Michelle said: "I gotta go," and left the pressroom.

I found out later that she had gone to the game room in the clubhouse and sat in a large plastic bubble and fired an AK-47 at a video screen where swarms of crazed Jihadists were rushing toward her.

When Paula Jean, the Clambake leader, entered the pressroom, I saw a more mature-looking teenager than I'd watched on the golf course. Curvy. Tan. Blond.

I don't usually ask questions in front of a group, but I said, "Paula Jean, you and Michelle put on quite a show today. Want to talk about it?"

Paula Jean said, "M.J. really stuck it today. I thought she was gonna shake the tree, but she cratered on the greens."

Somebody said, "It looks like a two-way battle between you two."

"No way," Paula Jean said. "There's a whole crew of SoKos behind us."

"The South Koreans, you mean," Emily said.

"Yeah. They're pretty killer."

The writer from *Teen Vogue* said, "Aren't some of the Oriental players from Japan and China?"

Paula Jean shrugged. "Same thing."

Emily asked, "The, uh, SoKos . . . what is it they do best on the course?"

"They've got it all," Paula Jean said. "They can download it. I played a practice round with Hee Ho Ding, and she cold-jumped a four-iron 267 yards to 16."

Another question. Did Paula Jean have a favorite club in her bag?

"My three-comp."

Emily said, "Your what?"

"I guess you old people would call it a three-wood or three-metal," Paula Jean said. "It's a composite. You know, like, composite material. Titanium, carbon, uranium."

A writer wanted to know if she had a current boyfriend.

Paula Jean said, "Terry would be hot."

"Who is Terry?" Emily asked.

"Terry Cutter. He's the new Rory. You living on Jupiter? Listen, I'm gonna boogie on outta here. How far is the mall from here in my limo?"

Emily looked around for help.

Becky Tracy said, "About four miles."

"I'm there," Paula Jean said, and left.

I accepted Emily's invitation to attend a dinner party that evening in her home, which bordered the golf course. "Home" might not be the right word. It more closely resembled King Ludwig's castle in Bavaria.

The best view was from the south terrace. You could gaze down on number 16, last of the three island greens. Number 16 was the one with the Mount Rushmore sculpted into a tall cliff behind the green.

I say Mount Rushmore. The rock faces on the cliff were

those of Bobby Jones, Ben Hogan, Jack Nicklaus, and Big Jake Lewis.

The truth is, I had never heard of Big Jake Lewis. But I learned he was the man who developed the property and arranged for the golf course and Mount Rushmore to be built. The course and the Mount Rushmore were finished shortly before he went to prison for fraud.

Big Jake Lewis's name was spoken in reverence at the dinner party among the twelve guests, all of whom were local residents in various shades of pink, lime, and gold. One guest, a gray-haired man whose name, if I heard it right, was Floppy, said Big Jake Lewis never robbed anybody who couldn't afford to lose it, and if the feds had left him alone everybody would have gotten their money back. "Some people just hate golf," Floppy said.

Emily asked us to join hands while she said a prayer as the first course arrived. She asked the Lord to continue to bless wineries, fashion designers, Cadillacs, JPMorgan Chase, the game of golf, and please tell all the terrorists and liberals to show a little respect for rich people, who mean well.

Paula Jean and Michelle Janine came out for the last round dressed for action. They wore short skirts that showed a lot of leg and breast-hugging, navel-exposing T-shirts. Ponytails dangled out of the backs of their visors.

They both drove the first green, a downhill par-4 of 345 yards, and two-putted for birdies. Michelle Janine drew gasps from the gallery when she reached the par-5 6th with a driver and five-iron. She sank the 20-foot eagle putt to take a two stroke lead on Paula Jean.

Paula Jean pouted and bit her lip.

Michelle Janine Fox toyed with her diamond earring as she walked to the next tee.

Paula Jean got even at the 590-yard par-5 10th. She hammered her drive 310 yards over a pure wasteland and into the fairway, then put a high nine-iron on the green and rammed a 30-foot putt into the cup for an eagle.

"Nothing but throat," I heard her say as she walked off the green, toying with her own diamond earring on her ear.

Now tied, Paula Jean and Michelle Janine battled evenly all the way to the 17th tee, which was where they heard the roar for the chunky Hee Ho Ding.

The SoKo had been five strokes back starting the day, but she had birdied four holes in a row on the back nine, two of them with chip-ins, and now she'd holed out a two-iron shot at Mount Rushmore for an ace. She was suddenly leading the Clambake by one.

Paula Jean and Michelle Janine both parred the last two holes, and all they could do then was wait to see how Hee Ho Ding finished.

Presently the scoreboard told them the SoKo had parred 17.

"Dink," Paula Jean said.

The way Hee Ho Ding played the par-5 18th hole would be remembered as one of the most bizarre finishes in the Clambake's history. She skied her tee shot, shanked her second, topped her third, and pulled her fourth into the pond that guarded the green on the left. She could see the ball three inches beneath the surface and decided to try to hit it out.

She took a mighty swing with a sand wedge and made a tremendous splash, but out came the ball with a piece of mud on it. The ball and the mud sailed directly into the cup on the fly for Hee Ho Ding's par—and her one-shot victory.

"Hog," Michelle Janine said.

"Bacon bitch," Paula Jean said.

A moment later I wheeled my cart around and drove to the pressroom. I finished the piece in an hour and went to the *Teen Vogue* hospitality tent to say good-bye to Emily Turner.

I found her dipping into a large vodka martini on the rocks. Perhaps her third or fourth. "It was a good show," I said.

"Yes," she said, slurring her words. "I'm sure all the little people in Seoul are happy."

I left for the airport in a taxi, opened my laptop, and read the story I'd filed. I think I did an okay job expressing my feelings about women's golf. My lead read:

"Does anyone really want to live in a world where the cutest girls don't win golf tournaments?"

THE NEXT BIG THING

Brazos State Teachers College for Men and Women announces that its women's golf program has signed Wanda Gaynelle Stout to a National Letter of Intent.

A native of Swamp Fever, Florida, Stout is ranked sixty-seventh nationally by *Golfscoop* magazine, trailing thirty-five ladies from Asia and the rest from California. She is also ranked twenty-seventh in the world by the Association of Daddies of American Junior Girls, which does not include international players.

Brazos State coach Edna Fay Taylor said, "Wanda Gaynelle is six-two and will fit in perfectly with our previously announced recruits from Finland, Croatia, Lichtenstein, and Turkey. I am confident this group can take our program to the next level. Each lady is tall, and most of them speak English."

Stout was named *Deep Divot Weekly's* Girl Player of the Year in 2012 when she won three tournaments—the IO2JG Junior Girls Invitational at Crab Shack Country Club near Destin, Florida, the FTJ3-17 Junior Girls Classic at Secret Quarry near Ocala, Florida, and the AIJG4M Junior Girls Match Play at Spring Break CC near Ponte Vedra Beach, Florida.

Wanda Gaynelle first caught everyone's attention in 2011 as a fourteen-year-old when she tied for medalist honors with two golfing gymnasts from Bucharest, Romania, at the World Girls 14-and-Under Juniors on Pinehurst No. 16.

The question of how Wanda Gaynelle is still listed as fourteen years old today continues to baffle followers of junior girls golf. Coach Taylor, however, said it is a nonissue, "a spike mark on the bent greens of life."

Stout's greatest achievement may well have been her victory in the 2013 Florida 2XA-52 State Championship at Blinding Sand Golf Links near Vero Beach. She was four under par through thirteen holes in the final round—and holding a slight lead—when the tournament was shortened by Hurricane Gwendolyn.

Coach Taylor said, "Wanda Gaynelle is one of the best junior golfers in the country and competes with a fire to win, especially when her tee ball finds the fairway."

Wanda Gaynelle inherited her love for the game from her father, Bo Boy Stout, a former professional golfer. Bo Boy achieved six top-twenty finishes in his playing days on the Fast Pencil Tour, which is now the Web.com Tour, and was previously the Ben Hogan Tour, the Nike Tour, the Buy .com Tour, and the Nationwide Tour.

Stout was homeschooled in Swamp Fever from the first grade through the ninth, mostly by golf magazines. She received a scholarship to the Academy of Gurus in the Everglades. It consists of an 18-hole course, dormitory, clubhouse, practice range, and storage bin for bug spray.

At an early age Wanda Gaynelle's father put a bucket-head driver in her hands and taught her to swing as hard as possible at the alligators that frequently crawled onto the family's front porch to devour empty beer cans.

Bo Boy was recently quoted as saying, "I knew I had me something when I seen her airmail a gator's jawbone onto the next boat dock. Me and her stepmama Francine are gonna ride this hoss all the way from college to the LPGA Tour."

DESTINATIONS

AMONG THE MANY things that have sneaked past me while my back was turned are these new public courses that are springing up across America—challenging, well manicured, painstakingly remote. They provide landing strips and boutique hangars for private jets and tree-lined drives leading up to fashionable clubhouses with elegant bars and restaurants in which you will find the most serious and adventurous recreational golfers that God ever poked in the ribs with a Callaway X Hot fairway composite with a modern warbird sole and a forged speed frame face cup.

It's certainly alien to what I once knew and considered normal—the rock-hard fairways, scrawny trees, dirt bunkers, and fuzzy greens of Goat Hills, the thieves sitting on the concrete porch in old rocking chairs waiting for the next sap to show up with money in his pocket, not to mention the greasy meatloaf at the lunch counter that passed for our men's grill.

But in today's world, the golf victim can travel far and wide to play public courses with fetching names and enjoy the fellowship of other golf victims.

Here are three places I'm happy to recommend:

Old Humbler at Salt Water Gulch

A difficult course within sight of eight drilling rigs producing natural gas in an obscure yet booming area of North Dakota.

The course has a plethora of Church Pews, Hell Bunkers, Redans, and Hogan Bridges. Par is between 75 and 80, depending on the time of year.

Three holes—the 3rd, 9th, and 14th—require a horseback ride from green to tee, but it's worth the effort to see the mounds where a dozen frozen drilling superintendents are buried.

Once you've enjoyed the golf course, ask Camille, the shapely bartender, to make you a Four-Putt cocktail, then savor a Roughneck Burger on pita with refried beans, chipotle, and snails, one of Chef Timothy's specialties.

Gun Creek Run at Wild Orchard Mountain

Although the course is not that far from Atlanta, it isn't easy to find unless you know your Civil War history and are skilled at hacking through brush.

The design outdoes itself by paying homage to the Baffling Brook, the Postage Stamp, the Alps, and the Cape. Each hole is named for a Confederate general. There is one rule that some visitors may find inconvenient. You must wear gray or butternut. Slacks, shirts, and sweaters of these colors are available for purchase in the pro shop.

Gun Creek's director of golf, Shorty Grits, is always available to assist you.

After your round, implore the shapely bartender, Celeste, to make you a Jeb Stuart cocktail to go with Chef Simon's Beauregard Burger, which is a rare possum pattie with turnip greens and eggplant on a sweet potato bun.

The Links of Squatting Screech Owl
This jewel of the Great Northwest wanders along a strip of land jutting into the Pacific Ocean off the coast of Oregon.

The best access is to be tendered to shore from a U.S. Navy destroyer.

The layout sets a high bar for originality. It was designed by a relatively unknown architect, Dippy Baker, who won a *Golf Digest* contest for design. The highlight might be the 18th hole, which presents a challenging finish.

This par-5, which is named The Scissors, stretches 896 yards over hill and dale and fishing pier. There are several options. You don't really know if you're hitting in the right direction until you find yourself on the green.

Phil Mickelson, I was told, currently holds the course record with a 78.

Collette, the shapely bartender, fixes a mean Albatross cocktail, and it goes down well with Chef Nigel's Reef Burger. He blends prime shark's belly with delicate chunks of squid, crisp minnows, and pureed spinach.

———

Between you and me, the things I've mentioned make me yearn for the old lunch counter at Goat Hills. Sure, the meatloaf might have been made of finely ground spare tires, but I ate it if there was enough A.1. left in the bottle.

At breakfast you needed to tell the cook, a tired man named Will, to put the trichinosis bacon back in the skillet and cook it till you couldn't see through it.

I would caution that around any public course, you are likely to find vultures loitering. It was at Goat Hills that I learned never to bet with a man in a hard hat who smoked Camels, never bet with a man in torn jeans with keys on his belt, never bet with a man with only five clubs in his bag, never bet with a man wearing an eye patch, and, needless to say, never bet with a man in suspenders and a Schlitz cap who says he will putt only with his nine-iron.

You may consider this last paragraph a public service announcement.

"MATCH OF THE CENTURY"

WALTER HAGEN IS known to have said, "You are only here for a short time—be sure to stop and smell the flowers." It is also known that Walter, as often as possible, stopped to smell the money.

It didn't take long for Hagen to figure out that he could bank more money in exhibition matches than he could by winning the Asheville-Biltmore Open, or something of that nature, on what constituted a haphazard PGA Tour in the early twenties, which happened to be the prime of Walter's silk-shirt life.

If another pro golfer had any sort of recognizable name, and was standing still, Hagen's manager, Bob Harlow, a man ahead of his time, might enlist him for an exhibition match.

Most of the exhibitions were 18-hole affairs, Hagen against the likes of Macdonald Smith, Leo Diegel, Bobby Cruickshank, "Wild Bill" Mehlhorn, Joe Turnesa, Emmett

French, Al Espinosa, or any other competitor whose name was vaguely familiar to the public.

It was in 1922 that Hagen and Harlow began to think big. A young upstart named Gene Sarazen won the U.S. Open at Skokie and the PGA at Oakmont that year, thus a "World Championship" match was arranged between Sarazen and Hagen. They played 36 holes in Pittsburgh and 36 holes in New York. Walter won the engagement 3 and 2.

In 1924 when Cyril Walker won the U.S. Open at Oakland Hills and Hagen won both the British Open at Hoylake and the PGA at French Lick, Harlow arranged a "World Championship" bout at 72 holes in Florida. Hagen dusted Cyril Walker 16 and 15.

Hagen would take his game global and win such tournaments as the French Open, the Belgian Open, and the Pan-American Exposition Open. In his travels he managed to work in a couple of "World Championship" battles with England's match-play specialists, Abe Mitchell and Archie Compston. He whipped Mitchell and split with Compston.

In 1928, after Johnny Farrell had won the U.S. Open at Olympia Fields in Chicago and Hagen had won the British Open at Sandwich, they played a "World Championship" series in five different cities—New York, Chicago, Detroit, Philadelphia, and St. Louis. Hagen won three of the five.

But in the middle of all that, Hagen and Harlow came up with their greatest promotion.

In late February 1926, a head-to-head match was arranged between Walter Hagen, the ruler of pro golf, and Bobby Jones, the ruler of amateur golf.

Hagen versus Jones, as you may guess, caused looks of gleeful anticipation.

At the time, Hagen was thirty-four years old and had won two U.S. Opens, two British Opens, and three PGAs. Jones was only twenty-three but had already won a U.S. Open and two U.S. Amateurs, and had been runner-up in two other U.S. Opens.

Bob Harlow, with help from his friends in the press, not only promoted the affair as a 72-hole "World Championship" but, more important, he sold it as "The Match of the Century."

Harlow somehow managed to raise a prize of $10,000 that would go to the winner, which of course would be Hagen since Jones was an amateur and couldn't accept prize money. But this didn't detract from the buildup.

Leading up to the match, numerous members of the sportswriting lodge ran away with themselves. They saw it as more than a golf game. It was going to be a Civil War, the North against the South—Hagen coming from Rochester, New York, Jones from Atlanta. It would be a class struggle. Hagen was a poor guy who had worked for every paycheck, while Jones was a country club kid from a well-to-do family, a borderline socialite. It would be a clash of cultures. Hagen played golf for a living, Jones played it "for the love of the game." So they wrote.

A majority of the sportswriters favored Jones, and it apparently didn't bother them that Hagen and Harlow had chosen the venues. The first 36 holes would be played at Whitfield Estates in Sarasota, Florida, a new course designed by Don-

ald Ross that would become known as the exclusive Sara Bay
Country Club. A week later the second 36 would be played
at Pasadena Golf Club near downtown St. Petersburg, Florida, a course designed by Hagen himself and two other guys.
That course has since been redesigned by Bill Dietsch and
then by Arnold Palmer and his partner Ed Seay, and is now
known as the Pasadena Yacht & Country Club.

A photo taken of Jones and Hagen on the first tee before
the match got under way on February 28 shows both titans
nattily dressed. Jones is wearing a shirt and tie, a long-sleeve
slipover sweater, plus-fours, and a fedora, and he holds a
cigarette in his hand. Hagen, bareheaded, is in a silk shirt
and tie, a sleeveless sweater, plus-fours, a pair of custom-
màde golf shoes, and his black hair is slicked down in the
fashion of Rudolf Valentino or a member of New York's
Café Society.

The match started off with Jones playing beautifully,
hitting fairways and greens, and Hagen hooking into the
trees and rough, then hitting rescue shots and sinking putts.
Through twelve holes Hagen held a one-up lead despite
Jones's excellent tee-to-green play.

But Hagen and his putter didn't let up. He birdied the
13th, 15th, and 16th to go 4-up, lost one hole to Jones's birdie
at 17, but ended the first 18 holes 3-up. That wouldn't have
been a steep hill to climb for Jones, except in the afternoon
Hagen fired a 69 by holing everything he looked at, putts
that ranged from 20 to 60 feet. He took a shocking 8-up
lead.

Jones had a week to let Walter's putter cool off before
the next 36 holes at the Pasadena Golf Club. An article

written on the match by Connor T. Lewis, at the request
of the USGA Golf Museum, reveals that the *Sarasota Her-
ald* hadn't given up on Bobby Jones. It printed the following
headline: "Miracles Can Happen, and the Par Assassin Is
Still Far from the Beaten Golfer."

Jones got away to a good start on March 6 by parring
the first two holes, and with Hagen 50 feet away for his par
at the second, he had every reason to think he was going
to cut into Walter's lead—with plenty of golf left. That's
when Hagen drained the 50-footer for a halve. Jones lowered his head in disappointment while Walter joked with the
gallery.

Hagen went on to take a 12-up lead through five holes,
and laughingly showboated his way to his famous victory,
12 and 11. It was the worst defeat of Bobby Jones's career.

The result led to this quote by Jones:

> I would rather play a man who is straight down the
> fairway with his drive, on the green with his second,
> and down in two putts for his par. I can play a man like
> that at his own game, which is par golf. If one of us can
> get close to the pin with his approach, or hole a good
> putt, all right. He has earned something. But when a
> man misses his drive, misses his second shot, and then
> wins the hole with a putt . . . well, it gets my goat!

Walter Hagen used the $10,000 in style. He donated
$5,000 of it to the St. Petersburg Hospital, and spent much
of the balance to buy Jones a pair of diamond cuff links.

Jones was left to say, "Walter, you've now ruined me

twice. First, you gave me this licking, and now I'll be busted the rest of my life trying to buy shirts to go with this jewelry."

You could say that Jones eventually had his revenge on Hagen after losing "The Match of the Century."

It's one of the more curious oddities in golf that Walter Hagen never won a major championship that Bobby Jones played in.

THE GREATEST ROUNDS

N CERTAIN CIRCLES the subject of golf's greatest rounds comes up, usually in step with adult beverages. I tend to dominate the conversation, basically because I am old enough to recall that the six-iron used to be called a spade-mashie.

Today I've decided to put the discussion to rest. After careful rummaging through Herbert Warren Wind, and calling on my own memories of the rounds I've covered with my own typing fingers, I've settled on a list.

Guidelines were established. The round had to be shot in a major championship, otherwise it would not be worth its weight in Argyle socks. It helped if the round went a long way toward winning a major.

Here, then, in chronological order, are the heroes who shot the greatest rounds and where and when they did it:

———

Francis Ouimet on September 20, 1913, at The Country Club in Brookline, Massachusetts. Boston to me. That day the unknown twenty-year-old amateur won the U.S. Open in a playoff over Harry Vardon and Ted Ray. It turned into a cakewalk. Ouimet shot a 72. Vardon shot 77, Ray 78.

The Open had been scheduled for June that year but was moved to September so the two famous Englishmen could arrange their travels in order to compete. Ouimet's stunning victory put golf on the front page of newspapers everywhere. I hadn't been born yet.

Walter Hagen on August 20, 1914, at Midlothian Country Club, eighteen miles southwest of Chicago. The flamboyant Hagen burst on the scene when he fired a four-under 68 in the opening round of the U.S. Open. It was the first sub-70 round in the Open's history. It sent Walter on his way to a one-stroke win over Chick Evans, an amateur star likewise on the rise. I still wasn't born yet.

Bobby Jones on July 12, 1930, at Interlachen Country Club in Minneapolis. Jones won four U.S. Opens, but this 68 was the lowest round he ever shot in the Open, and only the second time he broke 70. It came in the morning round of the 1930 Open when he brought it home in four under par.

That round gave Jones the cushion he needed to hold off Macdonald Smith in the afternoon and win by two strokes to capture the third leg of his Grand Slam.

I was one year old and remember it well.

Gene Sarazen on June 25, 1932, at Fresh Meadow Country Club in Flushing, Long Island, which is now gone. Sarazen's four-under 66 came in the last round of the '32 U.S. Open. He was actually four under over the last 36 holes, which enabled him to run away from Bobby Cruickshank and Phil Perkins and win by three strokes. Gene's 66-70 on the last day was considered a rare feat.

He joined Bobby Jones as the second player to win the U.S. and British Opens in the same year. The feat has been equaled since Sarazen's day only by Ben Hogan, Lee Trevino, Tom Watson, and Tiger Woods.

Henry Cotton on June 28, 1934, at Royal St. Georges Golf Club, Sandwich, England. Cotton started becoming the finest English golfer since Harry Vardon by ending the eleven-year dominance of Americans in the British Open. He did it at Sandwich by breaking all kinds of records, in particular his scorching 65 in the second round. It helped him to a five-stroke victory. Cotton would win two more British Opens in his career, in '37 at Carnoustie and '48 at Muirfield. But his round at Sandwich was the one that inspired the Dunlop 65 golf ball.

The first golf ball I ever swung at, I'm certain.

Byron Nelson on April 13, 1942, at the Augusta National. For all his other accomplishments—the win streaks and such—Byron himself always said that the three-under 69 he shot that day was the best golf he ever played. It won him the Masters in a historic playoff with Ben Hogan, who shot a 70.

What made it special was that Ben led Byron by three strokes through the first five holes, but Nelson shot five under par over the last thirteen holes for the win.

Ben Hogan on June 19, 1942, at Ridgemoor Country Club in Chicago. On this day Hogan shot a 10-under-par 62, which is still the lowest 18 ever shot in a major championship. It helped sweep Hogan to victory in an event officially called the Hale America National Open, now most often referred to as the U.S. "wartime" Open.

It is still debated as to whether this is Hogan's "fifth" Open—but not by Ben, or me. There was USGA regional qualifying and USGA sectional qualifying, the event was conducted under USGA rules, and Ben received the same prize money as at any previous Open and a gold medal for the win that looks an awful lot like the other four.

Sam Snead on April 10, 1949, at Augusta National. Sam shot many low rounds in his six decades of competition, including a 60 on Old White at the Greenbrier, but his finest round in a major was his five-under 67 on the last day to win his first of three Masters tournaments. Sam made eight birdies in the round. He actually closed with a pair of 67s to come from five strokes back and win by three over Lloyd Mangrum and Johnny Bulla.

This was the first year a green jacket was slipped on the Masters winner.

Ben Hogan on June 16, 1951, at Oakland Hills Country Club in Detroit. If anyone was going to have two rounds on this list, you might have guessed it would be Hogan. This three-under 67 in the last round of the '51 U.S. Open has been called the greatest ever played in the heat of a major on the most difficult course ever devised by man, beast, or Robert Trent Jones. It gave Hogan his third Open, and in fact his third in a row. He'd won in '48 at Riviera and '50 at Merion, but missed '49, of course, due to that altercation with the Greyhound bus.

As brilliant as it was, the round could have been lower. Ben bogeyed the 3rd and 14th holes with three-putt greens before closing with birdies at 15 and 18. It was my first Open to cover, and I'm pleased to report that after Ben brought "the monster" to its knees, I was able to wrestle my typewriter to the ground and write a story.

Arnold Palmer on June 18, 1960, at Cherry Hills Country Club in Denver. Show me a man who doesn't know what Arnold did in the last round of the '60 U.S. Open at Cherry Hills and I'll show you a soccer fan in Uruguay.

It was a six-under 65 that won Palmer the Open over Jack Nicklaus and Ben Hogan, a confluence of three kings of the fairway—past, present, and future. He came from fourteen players and seven strokes back in that final round.

Johnny Miller on June 17, 1973, at Oakmont Country Club in Pittsburgh. Miller came from only six strokes and twelve players back with his eight-under-par 63 in the last round of that U.S. Open.

Miller passed such competitors as Jack Nicklaus, Arnold Palmer, Lee Trevino, Julius Boros, and Tom Weiskopf by going out early and getting to the clubhouse ahead of the traffic.

Tom Watson on July 9, 1977, at Turnberry Golf Club in Ayrshire, Scotland. It was in this British Open, the first ever held amid the sea views of Turnberry, that Watson and Jack Nicklaus engaged in the greatest two-man duel in the history of majors. After they both shot 65s in the third round, Watson's five-under 65 in the fourth narrowly edged Jack's 66 to give him the claret jug.

Watson's 72-hole score of 268 broke the record, as did Nicklaus's 269.

Hubert Green, the reigning U.S. Open champion, finished third at 279, eleven strokes back of Watson and ten strokes back of Nicklaus, and said:

"I won the British Open. I don't know what tournament Tom and Jack were playing."

Gary Player on April 9, 1978, at the Augusta National. As the final round of this Masters began, Gary trailed the leader, Hubert Green, by seven strokes, and a group of eight other competitors that included Tom Watson, Lee Trevino, Hale Irwin, Gene Littler, and Tom Weiskopf.

All the South African did to win his third green jacket and his ninth, and last, major at the age of forty-two was shock the community by firing an eight-under 64. The round didn't look like much for more than an hour and a half, but Gary implausibly birdied seven of the last ten holes!

Jack Nicklaus on April 13, 1986, at the Augusta National. It's no news bulletin that Jack won so many major championships that it takes four hands to count them. None, however, aroused more emotion than this victory for his sixth Masters and eighteenth professional major at the age of forty-six.

Jack did it with a totally unexpected seven-under-par 65 in the last round that saw him make up four strokes and pass seven guys.

As Jack trudged triumphantly up the last fairway, you couldn't find a dry eye on the course, except maybe on Greg Norman and Tom Kite, who tied for second one stroke back.

Seve Ballesteros on July 18, 1988, at Royal Lytham & St. Annes. The Spaniard who rejuvenated European golf, and didn't do a bad job of livening up things in the United States, saved his greatest round for the last day of this British Open, and won the last of his five majors. It was a seven-under 65 to overtake the 36- and 54-hole leader Nick Price, and it came on the same course where he'd taken his first major in '79.

Seve was nicknamed the "Car Park Champion" by the press because he continually had trouble getting his tee shots in the fairways but also displayed an uncanny ability to recover and make pars and birdies.

"I don't aim for the rough," he said. "It just goes there."

Greg Norman on July 18, 1993, at Royal St. Georges Golf Club, Sandwich, England. Greg set a record for meltdowns and bad luck in the majors during his prime, but this was one week when he was unbeatable. He not only carried off his second British Open, but did it with a flawless eight-under 64 in the final round. He broke the 72-hole record with a 267, and needed every bit of it to hold off Nick Faldo by two strokes.

Tiger Woods on June 15, 2000, at Pebble Beach Golf Links, near Carmel, California. You could select any of three rounds Tiger shot in this U.S. Open as he shredded the record books and won by fifteen strokes. His seven-under 65 on opening day was low for Thursday. His three-under 69 on Friday was the only sub-70 round of the day. And his closing five-under 67 on Sunday was the best in the field. All week Tiger's game and putting were genius. His talent was at its peak.

I choose his opening 65. It caused heads to swim and jaws

to drop and got him off and running on his way to trampling a legendary golf course.

Phil Mickelson on July 21, 2013, at Muirfield Golf Links, Gullane, Scotland. After inflicting so many wounds on himself to finish runner-up in six U.S. Opens—including the one at Merion one month earlier—Phil played one of the great final rounds ever in a major with his winning 66 on the punishing and bewildering moonscape of Muirfield in the British Open.

That round of five under brought him from five shots and seven players behind—two of whom were Tiger Woods and Adam Scott.

I gladly place it among the five greatest rounds I've covered. In there with Ben Hogan at Oakland Hills in '51, Arnold Palmer at Cherry Hills in '60, Johnny Miller at Oakmont in '73, and Jack Nicklaus at Augusta in '86.

I might add that I will resent in the strongest possible terms any insinuation that this particular choice was influenced by the fact that I cashed a winning ticket on Phil for a handsome stack of coin.

In forty-five years of covering British Opens and visiting betting shops, it was about time I had a winner.

Finally, let me say that if I've overlooked or omitted somebody's round you admire, feel free to call and complain about it whenever the two of us happen to be in Dobrich, Bulgaria, at the same time.

GREATEST MOMENTS

A GREAT MOMENT IN golf may obviously be an 18-hole round, but it may also be a spectacular shot, a stunning result, a streak, a season, an interlude, an escapade, the way you wear your hat, the way we danced till three.

That said, I will now set about choosing golf's eighteen greatest moments. To do this I shall rely on personal memories, considerable research, depth of thought, and a heavy dose of opinion.

While little things may mean a lot in other aspects of life, they won't here. You won't find Mary, Queen of Scots swinging a shepherd's crook for the first time, or the persimmon driver being replaced by the Graf Zeppelin, or Tour wives becoming cuter through the years, having discarded matronly wardrobes and needlepoint on the verandas.

I will instead lean toward moments that have squeezed

into the lore of the game, bought a condo, and live happily within sight of an ocean, a mountain range, or a bent green.

The first three are gimmes. The others follow in no discerning order.

- Bobby Jones and the Grand Slam thing in 1930. A moment that started in June and ended in September.
- Ben Hogan's Triple Crown in 1953. Rivals Jones's Slam. Overall, Ben won five of the six pro tournaments he entered that year.
- Byron Nelson's streak and stockpile of wins in 1945. Not for nothing did he become known as "golf's mechanical man."
- Arnold Palmer becomes Arnold Palmer in the Masters, and keeps on being Arnold Palmer through U.S. Opens, revives the British Open. Takes golf to the masses.
- Ben Hogan's comeback in 1950 from the near-fatal automobile crash in 1949. Takes golf to the movies.
- Jack Nicklaus wins a sentimental sixth Masters and eighteenth professional major in 1986. Takes golf to the Kleenex box.
- Francis Ouimet's upset win over Harry Vardon and Ted Ray in the 1913 U.S. Open at Brookline. A young amateur startles the world, takes golf to the front pages.
- Gene Sarazen's double eagle in the 1935 Masters. Makes the four-wood a household necessity.
- Tiger Woods arrives.
- Sam Snead's horrendous 8 on the last hole that cost him

the 1939 U.S. Open at Spring Mill in Philadelphia—and his other Open losses to follow. Most negative fame a golfer ever received.

- Babe Zaharias takes up golf. Ladies who play the game enjoy increased acceptance. The LPGA is born in 1950.
- Nature creates the Old Course at St. Andrews, which, in turn, creates the cashmere sweater and travel agents.
- Gary Player's years of success and competitiveness. Continually gives needed PR to his homeland of South Africa.
- Lee Trevino bursts onto the scene by winning the U.S. Open of 1968 at Oak Hill in Rochester. Lee livens up the Tour for the next twenty years or longer.
- Tom Watson outlasts Jack Nicklaus in a two-day sub-par battle for the 1977 British Open at Turnberry. No birdies left for anyone else.
- Seve Ballesteros hand-carries golf around the European continent, achieves stardom in the United States, re-invents the Ryder Cup.
- Lew Worsham holes out a miraculous wedge shot on the last hole at Tam O'Shanter—and on national TV—to win the All American Open in 1953, which causes commentator Jimmy Demaret to blurt out over the air, "The son of a bitch went in!"
- Harry Vardon tours the United States for the first time in 1900, helps popularize the game by showing duffers how to grip the club and where the Vs should point, and demonstrating that the golf swing need not resemble a vicious cut with a baseball bat.

Emergency Nine

- President Dwight Eisenhower finally makes a par on the 12th at Augusta National, declares golf the national pastime.
- Technology helps make bad golfers better.
- Astronaut Alan Shepard hits a golf ball on the moon.
- Ben Hogan fires a fantastic 67 to win the U.S. Open in the final round at Oakland Hills in 1951. Greatest round on the toughest Open course in the history of mankind.
- Walter Hagen wins his fifth PGA Championship, and fourth in a row, at Cedar Crest in Dallas in 1927. An awed teenager in the gallery named Byron Nelson chooses golf as his favorite sport over baseball.
- John McDermott becomes the first American to win the U.S. Open in 1911 at Chicago Golf. Helps promote the growth of the game.
- The PGA Tour is organized in 1929 after years of bouncing around and passing the hat.
- TV slowly works up to covering all 18 holes of the majors.
- Mickey Wright swings a golf club like most guys would like to.

Three-hole Loop to Get Even

- Pine Valley happens. Founded in 1913, it evolves into the world's greatest golf course. Still is.
- Golf discovers the unmatched beauty of the Monterey

Peninsula after World War One. Begets Pebble Beach
and Cypress Point.

- The slipover shirt goes to golf in the early forties, sen-
tencing all dress shirts and neckties to Henry Picard's
closet.

TOP GURU

LOOK AT BUTCH Harmon, I see his dad. I listen to Butch Harmon, I hear his dad. Claude Harmon was my friend and the smartest man I ever knew about the golf swing. No wonder that Butch learned enough from his father to incorporate the wisdom into his own teachings and consistently find himself voted the number-one golf instructor west of Vladivostok, north of the Falklands, and due south of David Leadbetter.

It's impossible to talk about Butch—Claude Harmon Jr.—without talking about his dad, the 1948 Masters champion, the last club pro to win a major. Claude Harmon didn't tell golf stories, he told opinions. He had plenty of them, and most of them were on-target. Nobody understood this better than Butch.

I used to seek out a seat at a table next to Claude in the Augusta National clubhouse every spring during the Masters to soak up his tales and opinions, often told with a sweep of his hand.

We had Ben Hogan in common as a friend and idol.

Claude would say, "Ben Hogan would rather let a black widow spider crawl inside his shirt than hit a hook." Then he would add, "It's not the hook that kills you, it's the fear of hitting it."

Today you might guess it came from Claude if you hear Butch say, "You don't practice a golf swing, you practice golf *shots*. If you aim at nothing, you'll hit it every time."

I once asked Butch if I could tell him a story about his dad that he might not have heard.

Butch grinned. "You start it, I'll finish it."

I can still hear Claude saying, "If a man tells me he knew President Eisenhower, I would ask him how President Eisenhower liked his steaks cooked. I know how Ike liked his steaks cooked—with a layer of salt on both sides. And he liked a sliced onion sandwich on light bread with mustard. Good for the heart. I knew Ike. I taught Ike."

Claude also taught Kennedy, Nixon, and Ford, not to overlook Howard Hughes, Bob Hope, Bing Crosby, Henry Ford, the Duke of Windsor, and King Hassan II of Morocco.

Doing a magazine piece, I was once with Claude on one of his trips to Morocco. I wasn't permitted to dine or socialize with the king, but I followed him as he played golf on a course inside the walls of one of his palaces. King Hassan II might have been Claude's toughest golf pupil.

In the city of Fez one evening as we dined on barbecued goat, Claude said, with a sweep of the hand, "It's not easy to explain to His Majesty that the golf club doesn't know he's a king."

Butch can drop the names of some of his own important students, past and present. To name four: Tiger Woods, Phil Mickelson, Greg Norman, and Ernie Els.

Tiger won his first eight pro majors with Butch Harmon. Butch didn't try to do anything with Tiger's swing. He mainly spoke to him about course management and how to conduct himself around the people he would be dealing with.

How much to tip locker room attendants, hotel housekeepers, restaurant help, anyone who does him a favor. All that, along with how to activate his credit cards.

Butch explained to Tiger that he should make an attempt to be cordial and cooperative with the press. IMG, the agency that originally signed Tiger, evidently told him something else in that regard.

Butch hasn't needed to instruct Phil Mickelson on any form of generosity.

Phil has always been popular with the fans and press, and, as those in the know can attest to, he's a notorious big tipper. There's a host of locker room guys, hotel maids, waiters, waitresses, and maître d's who will testify to his generosity.

When Butch was a kid running around trying to learn the game, Claude was the "head coach at Harmon Tech," officially known as Winged Foot Golf Club. If you wanted to play a medley of Claude's hits, the assistants who passed through "Harmon Tech" in those years included Jackie Burke, Dave Marr, Mike Souchak, Dick Mayer, Rod Funseth, and Al Mengert.

Butch was exposed to that, as were his three brothers—Craig, the head pro for over forty years now at Oak Hill in Rochester, New York; Billy, who is now the director of golf at Toscana Country Club in Palm Springs; and Dick, the longtime pro at River Oaks in Houston who shockingly passed away a few years ago.

Winged Foot was special back then. It had a dazzling membership. Some of the best known were Tommy Armour; Fred Corcoran, who once ran the PGA Tour and was the agent for Sam Snead and Ted Williams; Dick Chapman, who won both the U.S. Amateur and British Amateur; Frank Gifford, the football hero and TV broadcaster; and finally Craig Wood, the 1941 U.S. Open and Masters champion who became a member after he retired as Winged Foot's head pro. Claude had been Wood's assistant and was put in line by Craig to become his successor.

Butch would argue that Winged Foot was the greatest club in America back then, a true sportsman's haven. But times have changed. Butch has observed a new breed of member now. The guy who goes from Choate to Yale to the first tee at Winged Foot West.

Golf's top instructor enjoys explaining how Claude tried to curb Butch's anger on the golf course when he was a young man.

After watching a youthful Butch throw a tantrum after shooting a 79 one day, Claude said to Butch, "I can see Arnold Palmer getting mad, but what have *you* got to be mad about? You're no good, anyhow."

Somehow I can hear Butch passing that along to someone whose game he's trying to help. It's in his DNA.

A CURE FOR BETRAYALS

HAVING HURLED MY share of seven-irons at benches and tree trunks when they sabotaged me in moments of financial crisis, I can tell you that nothing was better for the soul after a financially disappointing round than relaxing in bars, taverns, and hangouts.

In the confines of these sociable places I could have a Junior and water, maybe four, and dwell on what must have caused the day's tragedies to occur.

Why on my downswing at the 5th did I wonder if I'd put food down for the dog before I left the house?

Why when I stood over a putt at the 12th green was I still letting it bother me that my old school had named a new building on campus after a Marxist Commie Socialist pig?

Why, since there was water behind the green at the 9th, did I wonder if I had too much club on my takeaway?

Why, since there was water in front of the green at the 15th, was I thinking that my car needed an oil change?

Why, inasmuch as I feared my hook might return on the 18th tee, was I thinking that I had only one cigarette left in the pack, and I knew the machine in the clubhouse was broken?

I should have learned years earlier that golf is 90 percent mental once you know how to grip the club.

I should have learned it back when Spec Sims, the best gambler I ever knew, told me what had happened to him in a big-money match he gave away when he was one up with one to play.

Spec said when he stood over the two-footer for the win on 18, a win that would see a nice amount of whip-out make its way into his pocket, he realized as he stroked the putt that he hadn't been focusing on making it—he'd been thinking about Rita Hayworth in the movies.

He said it was the best golf lesson he ever learned the hard way.

Spec said, "You have to step on a man's throat, then you can think about Rita Hayworth when you get to the bar."

I used to enjoy the humor I'd find in the watering holes I'd frequent after a round. I enjoyed listening to the talk-big guys. I'd hear:

"People up East who like that TV show *Dallas* don't know the nearest cowboy hat to Dallas is thirty miles west in Fort Worth."

"We don't need A-rab oil. We got all the dinosaurs and whales we need right here in Texas."

"I'll worry about people freezing from no heat up in New York City when I see an offshore drilling rig sittin' next to the Statue of Liberty."

"Baby doll, I believe you can switch me to a glass of red. Wine don't count, does it?"

This takes me back to the days when a man could light a cigarette without finding himself surrounded by squad cars and fire trucks. In that day the citizenry drank Junior, Curtis, Jack, Crown, and Count Vod instead of Pellegrino.

I was back in Fort Worth for the Colonial and having a drink in the clubhouse with an old friend when our attention was drawn to the stand-up bar where a gentleman had been taken hostage by a smokin'-hot showstopper.

I estimated she'd just returned from a tristate crime spree of homewrecking.

"I know him," my friend said. "That's not his wife."

"I'm shocked," I said.

My friend said, "It looks like he's drinking himself invisible."

I said, "Yeah, he started out witty and charming and worked his way up."

Thus was born The Ten Stages of Drunkenness. They appeared in a novel I perpetrated, *Baja Oklahoma*. For these purposes I'll cut the stages down to five:

1. Witty and Charming
2. Rich and Powerful
3. Crank Up the *Enola Gay*
4. Invisible
5. Bulletproof

The list turned out to be popular. It turned up on the walls of bars, taverns, and grillrooms from Chicago to Atlanta, from Boston to Miami, from Houston to L.A.

I was flattered and would celebrate at P.J. Clarke's in Manhattan.

I'd sip my way to a final for the evening.

I'd have a grand final.

I'd have a grand majestic final.

I'd have a getaway.

I'd fake one more getaway.

I'd finally have a nightgown and be out of there.

And I survived.

Now I drink root-beer floats.

LETTER OF RESIGNATION

The secretary of a golf club in New England has
been dismissed for inappropriate behavior involving
alcohol and sexual harassment.

—NEWS ITEM

Dear Board of Governors and Members,

Surely all of you at Weeping Ruins Country Club know
how painful it is for me to write this letter of resignation. I
am dictating it to Nelda Reese, our dutiful secretary for
lo these many years. Weeping Ruins has been my life for
the past thirty years. I would bury myself in our deepest
bunker for this club. That would be the one left of 16 green,
of course.

How well I remember my first round of golf at the
Ruins. It was the day the water had receded on the back
nine after Hurricane Tina, which, ironically, was the name
of the first cart girl I married.

I played the East course that day. This was before we
took the 2nd, 3rd, and 7th from the North, the 5th from
the South, and the 13th from the West, and integrated
them into the East in an effort to host a U.S. Open.

I'm proud to have led the fight to make those changes.

Although the club has yet to attract the Open, I'm convinced the improvements have helped us continually draw a good field for the Weeper, our annual member-guest.

As I think back on my first round that day, how could I forget who was in the foursome with me?

Dr. Bob (Close 'Em Up) Sloan was there. He was rightfully proud of the fact that he could remove six gallbladders in a single morning and never miss his afternoon tee time.

There was Easy Ed Case, the prince of insurance. I think it's fair to say most of us got a kick out of Easy Ed telling us about the fine print he kept coming up with.

There was Knobby Thurber, four-time club champion, and a man I always thought was my friend until lately. Obviously he hasn't gotten over me dropping a bottle of vodka on his left foot a month ago. I can see how the accident might have affected his stance, as he so vigorously complained at the board meeting. But you would think Knobby would have had some sympathy for me. It was the finest potato vodka they make in Poland.

I want everyone to know I have apologized profusely to Rudy Conover, club president, for the joke I made about his wife. I mean, when she drowned in the pond left of 12. It was a reminder that you can never be too careful lining up a putt.

Anyhow, I thought it was obvious humor when I said it shouldn't have happened to an Exxon heiress, but at least Rudy had a good amount of the stock to remember her by.

Excuse me a minute. The old potato appears to be beckoning. A couple of swigs ought to smooth things out.

Now then. I want to explain in full about the incident

with Cindy, the new cart girl. As you know, Cindy is the younger sister of Tammy, the second cart girl I married—the one who left me for our tennis pro, "Rex the Wagon Tongue." I don't recall his real name. I do recall they are no longer together. I hear he parks cars now at a hotel in Naples, Florida, and she is a ski instructor in Dubai.

All I did while Cindy was pouring me a vodka rocks on the 11th fairweg . . . fairway . . . was ask if she had a valid placemat . . . passport. And I did suggest that she hadn't seen Capri until she'd seen it with fleas . . . with me.

I never laid a glove on Cindy, not that she would have allowed it after she watched me vomit on her sloose . . . shoes. And so, my friends, it is with a heavy heart that I tender this registration . . . resignation.

But I want everyone to know I have been forgiven for all of my past flavors . . . failures . . . by my wife, Noreen . . . Nadine . . . whatever. I now leave you with fawn . . . fond memories of our club's martini splashes . . . glasses.

Yours booley . . . truly.
Member #K-659

SO LONG, PARD

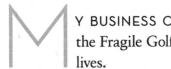Y BUSINESS CARD reads "Personal Shrink to the Fragile Golfer." It means what it says. I save lives.

A question I often hear from a client goes along these lines: "How can I get rid of the annoying jerk in my Saturday foursome that I have grown to despise? I'm afraid he's going to force me to commit a crime that'll land me in prison, and I don't want to go to prison. It would ruin my short game."

I have listened and learned that the annoying jerk may come in a variety of forms.

He is the man who says, "I still play Balata. I like to work the ball."

His golf shirts fit too tight.

He may favor orange shirts with green slacks, or pink shirts with yellow slacks, even though he's not color-blind.

He has been known to make twenty-two calls on his cell in nine holes.

He'll study a chip shot from four angles, then flub it.

He nods at you like he knew what you were going to say after you said it.

He occasionally will have you spend fifteen minutes looking for his second shot that's lost, then he will realize he hasn't hit it yet.

He likes to talk about his one trip to Scotland and recite the poem he's written about the Old Course.

He orders the popcorn soup.

He shows up with a new driver every two weeks, and says on the first tee, "Let the big dog eat." The big dog usually dines out of bounds.

He gains a minimum of one foot each time he marks his ball on the greens.

He thinks Pine Valley is a California wine.

Here are suggestions that may help you get rid of him:

Lose his golf ball every chance you get. When he's
    not looking, throw it over fences, into creeks, into
    bushes, on top of condos.
Gather a bunch of eight-by-ten gloss photos of
    Liberace. Autograph them to him and circulate
    them freely among the members, saying they were
    found in his locker. They can be tucked inside
    menus in the Fairway Dining Room.
Overwhelm him with swing tips. Tell him a new
    theory holds that the Vs should point to his left ear.
    Tell him the old idea of placing a newspaper under
    the right arm to keep the elbow close to the body

when practicing the swing works better with the Oxford English Dictionary.

Post nefarious notes on prominent walls in the clubhouse announcing that he is nine months delinquent on his bill.

Circulate the rumor that his real family name is Keitel and he is the distant cousin of Field Marshal Wilhelm Keitel. We all know what that name meant at the Nuremberg Trials.

Insist on driving when the two of you share a golf cart so you can take dangerous curves at high speed.

Walk abreast of him when crossing the bridge over the gorge at number 12 while keeping in mind that a gentle nudge can do the trick.

Tell him you've discovered a club maker in Cairo who makes drivers that guarantee incredible distance. The clubhead is made of the crushed skulls of Egyptian pharaohs. Provide an address. Google Earth can help here.

Casually mention that you saw his wife last week. She was strolling through the mall with a handsome, well-built young man in a muscle shirt and tight shorts.

Over the years these suggestions seem to have achieved the most success. It's why I get the big bucks.

THIEVES

MOST AMATEUR GOLFERS fall into two categories: those who cheat on their handicaps and those who don't. Those who cheat hold to the belief that you can never have too many silver trays, silver bowls, and silver pitchers in one home. Those who don't cheat have this fear that if they even consider the idea, God will steer them into freeway accidents that will leave them with incurable slices for the rest of their lives, if not, in fact, dead.

But handicap thieves provide for interesting discussions. A group of us came together the other day in the men's grill and talked about it.

We started when Rob dropped in and blinded us with his chest. Rob's chest was covered in gold coins on gold chains dangling around his neck. They were clearly visible, as his pirate shirt was unbuttoned to the waist.

The jewelry and shirt did not detract from his out-of-season tan, the obvious evidence of a face-lift, his Elvis pompadour, and his tight white slacks.

"Rob, it's the new you," somebody said.

"It goes better with my lifestyle," Rob said. "You know how many movie people I hang with when I hit the Coast."

"You're a sick man, Rob."

"Yo!" Rob said. "I'm invited to Pebble Beach . . . the Springs . . . Vegas four times a year. I know guys who'd kill for that."

"It doesn't bother you to take a 26 with you? We know you're a four."

"Man, everybody's a thief out there. You ought to see what the guys from Goldman Sachs bring."

Rob said he did have one problem. He'd met this babe in Carmel. She was hot. Really hot. They'd gotten involved. But the last time he was with her she told him the thing she admired most in a man was honesty. Rob couldn't decide whether to tell her about his wife and two kids.

I said, "I don't see how that's a problem for you, Rob. It's only a moral question."

"Hey, that's right," Rob said. "I'm cool."

Floyd recalled the time he was making business calls on customers and stopped by Rock Creek Muny on the other side of town. He thought he'd have a cup of coffee with Skeeter Morris, the head pro. Skeeter was an old buddy.

Floyd and Skeeter were sitting in the pro shop when this

guy came in. Skeeter introduced him to Floyd. His name was A.R. something.

"I don't know what it is, Skeeter," A.R. said, displaying an awkward practice swing. He had the flying elbow and a choppy finish.

He wore a rain hat, ragged jeans, a dingy golf shirt, and scuffed-up brown golf shoes.

He said, "I haven't broken 95 in six months. I can't find a fairway with an Indian guide. I hit every iron crooked. I wish I could get back to my 12, Skeeter. I can't come no closer to a 12 right now than I can to a pretty woman."

Skeeter said, "I'm tied up, but Floyd here is a good player. Maybe you can talk him into going nine with you . . . give you some pointers."

Floyd said it was a pretty day and he could put off making the rest of his calls. He got his clubs out of his car and met A.R. on the first tee.

A.R. said, "You know, as much as I love this game, I seem to try harder if I've got a little something going. What say you give me three up, and we play nine for a hundred, press to get even on the last hole if you need to."

Floyd looked the guy over. He was taking peculiar practice swings with an old persimmon driver. The clubhead took up turf once or twice. Floyd gave him the three up.

A.R. teed off first and striped it down the fairway with a much different swing. The drive went about 285.

"I'll be damned," A.R. said. "How in the world did that thing find the fairway? Luck was my friend that time."

Addressing his approach shot with a five-iron, he said,

"I never know what to expect with this club. Shank. Top. Scoop. Here goes nothin'."

The shot flew 165 yards, landed on the green, and settled in two feet from the flag.

"Whoa!" he yelled. "Where'd that come from?"

Floyd handed the guy a $100 bill, slid into his cart, and turned toward the clubhouse.

A.R. said, "You givin' up? Lot of holes left. You sure?"

Floyd said, "I've never been more sure of anything in my life."

Jim Ed joined us. He entered complaining.

"I'm fed up," he said. "I played my heart out last week in Houston. I ran the table on the greens for three rounds. My worst score was 68. I carried my partner the whole way. We finished 37 under. But guess what?"

"You came in twentieth," somebody said.

"Not even close," Jim Ed said. "It took 43 under to win . . . 39 under to get tenth. We didn't even win a pie plate. I'm tired of watching some diddy-bump drop-case who can't hit it out of this room walk off with all the hardware."

"What's your handicap now?" Floyd asked.

"They gave me a three there, but you know I'm scratch."

"There's your problem. You need a California handicap."

"How would I do that?"

Jim Ed was kind of naive.

Floyd said, "It would take a while, but it would be worth it to you. I know how much you love golf and how much you like to compete."

Jim Ed was told to play twenty rounds at the club with different people, but throw in disasters. Hit balls in the water. Hook drives out of bounds. Four-putt three or four greens. Stub as many chip shots as possible, but make it look accidental. Mix up the disasters with the good holes. Follow up a birdie with a hard-luck 10. Turn in a bunch of 85s and 87s. The pro would attest to his scores. He could be an 18 in no time.

Jim Ed looked excited.

"I'll do it!" he said. "I'll get me an 18. Then, by God, we'll see who can play this game and who can't."

THE PERFECT CLUB

S WAMP OR NO swamp?

That was my first dilemma. I was starting to design the perfect golf club for a group of wealthy Texans. They wanted a true links, and I was naturally aware that a true links in the United States has to be built on land reclaimed from a real estate developer.

There were other considerations.

Bulkheads or no bulkheads?

Waste areas or no waste areas?

Quarry or no quarry?

Greens that break toward the town houses, or greens that break toward Naomi's Cove.

Naomi was the wife of one of the wealthy Texans. She had always wanted her own cove. It would go with her private jet that can fly nonstop from anywhere in the world to Bergdorf Goodman in New York.

To save time I consulted with an architect who claimed to

know something about coves, town houses, and where the sun comes up and goes down.

When I tired of hearing him talk about drainage and grass and prevalent winds, I made it simple for him.

I said, "Just give me 7, 8, and 9 from Pebble, 12 and 13 from Augusta, the Road Hole from St. Andrews, and take the other 12 from Pine Valley, throw 'em up in the air, let 'em land where they want to."

With a project like this, some developers start with the golf course, some start with the hotel, some start with the casino. Or they go casino, hotel, golf course. It depends on the financing.

The investors wanted a hotel that was as understated as possible if you blended Windsor Castle with the Taj Mahal. I said if we went with the Taj, we might run into plumbing problems.

The hotel had to be sizable since the guests they hoped to attract would be bringing large groups for a week—their swing coaches, nurses, psychologists, lawyers, accountants, PR consultants, security, and food tasters.

I needed land as well. Land, lots of land, under starry skies above. Certainly enough land for the other activities— polo, hunting, fishing, boating, hiking, horseback riding, croquet, wandering.

Jogging will NOT be permitted within five miles of the property. Joggers sling sweat on innocent bystanders, and occasionally drop dead, which is inconvenient.

The hotel menu will be simple and tasty. Breakfast available twenty-four hours a day. Other all-day treats would be barbecue ribs, beef brisket, Tex-Mex, chili and rice, catfish, cheeseburgers, meatloaf, chicken and dumplings. Maybe some butter beans. Chefs from the finest truck stops in America will be brought in.

It goes without saying that the club will NOT host weddings, debutante parties, charity balls, Easter egg hunts, Fourth of July picnics, Halloween costume parties, Super Bowl parties, election night parties, New Year's Eve celebrations, seminars, or banquets of any nature.

Members and guests using cell phones anywhere but in their private rooms will risk physical torture and banishment from the grounds.

Employees, domestic or foreign, will be required to speak English at all times. Tipping the help is not required, but is encouraged. May the best man win.

No tee times are necessary, the course will never be crowded, and the club and golf course will be open 365 days a year. None of this silly holiday business.

There will be one other distinctive feature.

Storm shutters and steel walls on every structure will be activated instantly in case of violent weather approaching. In addition, snipers will be posted on the roofs at various points, in case any organized group of rejuvenated moron hippies and their commie professors from the faculty lounges might show up to insist that this land is their land.

It's time we got back to a civilized society again.

CELEBRITIES

ONCE UPON A time the Bing Crosby National Pro-Am was the most glamorous winter event on the PGA Tour. Every name pro entered, and every amateur was somebody who could act, sing, dance, and play golf well enough not to kill a spectator. This, of course, was before Bing passed away and some wry wit changed the name of the tournament to—I think I have this right—the AT&T National Pro-CEO & Corporate Boondoggle.

When Crosby Week came around every February, the Pebble Beach neighborhood, and every nook and cranny in smug yet picturesque downtown Carmel, would begin to be populated by a species known as Real Celebrities. These were people who happened to have accomplished something in sports or showbiz to justify such status.

It was a sane and joyful time in the world. There wasn't a Miley Cyrus or a Justin Bieber in it. Those were the days.

I was assigned—and it was my privilege—to cover fourteen Crosby tournaments from the late sixties through the early eighties. It is pure gossip that I covered them from a chair at the bar in Club XIX in the Pebble Beach Lodge, where I'd be staying, having no threshold for inconvenience.

You could have seen me out on number 8 and number 9 on Pebble from time to time to watch the suffering on those great par-4 holes. You could have seen me strolling around Cypress Point, to see what it was like to feel rich. I even went out to investigate Spyglass Hill to see why nearly every pro wanted it bulldozed.

I was invited to play in the Crosby a few times. Dave Marr invited me to be his amateur partner. Ben Crenshaw invited me to play as his partner. Even Kathryn Crosby, Bing's widow, invited me, and said she'd find me a pro. I always declined, having no fondness for five a.m. wake-up calls, freezing weather, blinding mist, and ice plant.

Besides, I wanted to be in my bar chair in Club XIX every evening. Well, every evening except one. That would be the night I'd let myself get talked into going to dinner with friends in smug yet picturesque downtown Carmel.

Someone would have made a reservation six months ahead in a small, hidden restaurant on a dark Carmel side street, chic but cramped, where the waitress would be dressed like a member of the Trapp family, and your fresh filet of Pacific red snapper would be served on a bed of tiny gold bracelets and emerald necklaces, or so the check would indicate.

There would occasionally be the opportunity to go to

exclusive old Cypress Point for lunch. One year my wife and I and another couple were taken by the attractive young wife of a member. But because she was wearing a designer pantsuit, we were denied admittance to the dining room. No pants allowed.

It didn't seem to matter to the maître d' that there was hardly anyone else in the dining room or, more important, that the lovely young wife happened to own Palm Beach, Florida.

"Give me a moment," she said to the maître d'.

She disappeared briefly, went to her car, then returned with her pants off and her raincoat tied around her waist.

"Will this do?" she said acidly to the maître d'.

"That will do nicely, madam," he said.

Then we had lunch.

An evening later, a group of us were dining at a place in Monterey. In the dinner party was my pal Don Cherry, the singer-golfer, who was playing in the Crosby. He listened to us talk about how good the food was at Cypress Point for a few moments, and said, "What's so good about a sandwich and an apple?"

I laughed out loud, realizing that the Crosby competitors in those days weren't allowed in the Cypress Point clubhouse when they played there in the rotation—they were given box lunches.

Back in the lodge, the bar chair was actually a stool with a backrest. Tom Oliver, the lodge manager then, did threaten at one point to put my name on a bronze plate on the backrest of the chair. This was because I was usually in there from seven till closing. I should explain that my chair was in the near corner on your right as you came down the stairs and entered what most people called the casual restaurant and I called tournament headquarters.

The longtime bartender, Chris Ursino, now late of this world, could handle everybody's refreshment needs while providing intellectual conversation with each serving.

It's where I would relax with my Winstons and young scotches and chat with friends and acquaintances who would stay for one cocktail, or several. I speak of pals like Dave Marr, Jack Whitaker, and baseball's greatest catcher, Johnny Bench, who knew more Kristofferson lyrics than I did. If I was in need of a movie star fix, I could always count on saying hello to George C. Scott—"Good to see you again, General"—and spending a fair amount of time in the presence of Jack Lemmon and James Garner.

It was a pleasure to discuss golf with Jack Lemmon.

"I did it today," he said one evening at the bar, swinging an imaginary club. "On number 7 at Pebble? Man, I caught it flush on the clubface. Gave it a really good whack. Like this—bam! I'm telling you, it felt good."

"Did you hit it close?" I asked.

"No," he said. "But it almost got airborne."

A heartwarming Crosby story goes back to the days when ABC televised the event. It involves two good buddies, the late Mac Hemion and the late Andy Sidaris, directors and producers under Roone Arledge's guidance.

Sidaris called Mac one morning to wake him up, to tell him what time everybody was expected to be on the tower at 18 for rehearsal, and Andy did a good job of imitating Bing Crosby's voice.

"Good mornin', Malcolm," Sidaris said. "The Old Groaner here. What time shall I discard the persimmon and croon a tune on the Good Ship Tower today?"

"Bite me, Andy," Mac said, hanging up and pulling the blanket over his head.

Presently, the phone rang again. Mac simply picked it up and slammed it back down.

A moment later the phone rang a third time. Mac picked it up and listened long enough to realize it was, in fact, the Old Groaner himself. Der Bingle.

"Jesus, Bing, it was you," Mac said. "Sorry."

"No problem, Malcolm," Crosby said. "Might I venture the guess you had a nice long visit with the juniper berry last evening?"

THE MERCHANDISE SHOW

THE ANNUAL MERCHANDISE show is always worth the trouble of fighting the crowds; you can load up on free stuff—golf balls, shirts, visors, ball markers, posters. I was in the drawing for the super range finder, the one that also shows TV channels, movies, and golf instruction, but I didn't win. I was lucky in another way, though. I got the last posters that were left of Blubber Oates and Frecklebelly Edwards, two of my favorite Tour players.

Every exhibit had new things to promote.

My first stop was at the golf cart booth. The cart was bright yellow. It was a four-seater with the steering wheel wrapped in a sable cover. It was equipped with air-conditioning and central heating with push-button windows and plush leather seats. The computer and TV were on the dash, and there was a microwave oven and foldout service bar in back.

A beautiful young model in a bikini was sitting in the cart.

I asked the exhibitor how much the cart was.

He said, "With or without Malya?"

"Who's Malya?"

"The young lady in the cart."

"She goes with the cart?"

"That would be up to you."

"How much is the cart by itself?"

"Right at twelve thousand, five hundred."

"How much with Malya?"

"Wait a second," the exhibitor said. He went to speak to Malya.

He returned and said, "A million four, but that's only for the first six months."

I said, "I'm not sure the missus would like having Malya underfoot. Is there something going on in the world of golf I don't know about?"

He said, "We're losing players, pal. Every year. The game's become too stodgy for the new generation. We're trying to keep the recreational golfers we have in this country, and attract new ones."

Malya smiled at me and tossed her hair.

The exhibitor said, "There's one other feature to this cart you may like. It goes up to seventy miles an hour."

"Why would I want to go seventy miles an hour in a golf cart?"

He said, "Let's say you've hooked your tee shot in the rough. You want to get to your ball before the others in your foursome, right? Give yourself a little better lie? All you do is use your right foot. You're there."

"I'll think about it," I said, and moved on.

A voice on the PA system announced that Stat Man Shields would be starting his lecture on his new golf scoring system on Aisle 6. I wandered over.

Stat Man Shields didn't seem to mind that there were only four of us in his audience. This included the six-month-old baby in a backpack on a man in shorts, T-shirt, and flip-flops who was practicing his putting stroke with a purchase he'd made earlier.

Stat Man Shields was saying, "This is the same system I've used to prove that Felix Serafin was a better golfer than Sam Snead … that Al Watrous had a better scoring average in the Open than Bobby Jones, and so on and so forth. You can't simply go by the score a golfer shoots if you want to know how well he's playing the game. There's more involved. One example. Does a putt that goes in from off the froghair count as much as a putt of the same length on the green? No. You subtract a half point. Another example. Does a drive in the first cut deserve the same two points as a drive of comparable distance in the fairway? No. Subtract one-fourth of a point if it's a par-5 hole, one half point if it's a par-4. Hitting the green on a par-3 is worth one point. Missing the green is no penalty unless you're in the water. When you add up all the points at the end of the day, and measure the total against the odds of thirty-six one-hundredths over fifty-five one-hundredths, you will have a good idea of what kind of round you shot. Questions?"

I had only one. "Who let you out?"

—————

THE PUTTER MAN. That was the sign on the booth. The proprietor could have passed for a Texas Ranger. He wore his Stetson barely above eye level. Pressed Western shirt, neatly creased jeans, ostrich boots.

On display was a variety of traditional putters. No bellies or broomsticks. Only old Armours, Cash-ins, Bullseyes, and Ted Smith Mallets. All of them in mint condition. Mixed in with the Pings, Camerons, Mortal Locks, what have you.

There was a decent crowd standing around. I managed to work my way up to the front row.

The Putter Man, who wore a Stetson and could pass for a ranch foreman, was holding up a Bullseye.

"Now, this dude," he said. "What I've got right here will get the job done. When the flash mobs come over the fence and onto the fairway to get your goods, you can take out the first wave by yourself. Pop, pop, pop, pop. Like that."

He went on. "The trigger on this dude is down on top of the blade. The shaft is loaded with nine-millimeter Golden Sabre 147 grain jacketed hollow points. You can get thirteen hundred feet a second at the muzzle."

I looked at the other people. They were absorbed.

I said, "All these putters you have are made into weapons, like guns?"

"You bet your sweet life, they are," he said. "I designed 'em myself and did the work. You must not be keepin' up with the news. In the past two months alone, we've had twelve robberies on golf courses right here in Northwest

Central Mid-Texas. The scum come out of nowhere. Sometimes they take more than your money; they drive off with the whole dern cart."

I asked what the police were doing about it.

"The police?" he said. "I'll tell you what the police is good for. When the police ain't causing traffic jams by stoppin' old ladies to check their IDs, they get a call about a break-in, go to the wrong address, and shoot an innocent man watering his front yard."

The Putter Man said there was another splendid use for his putters.

"With one of these," he said, "you can take care of the assistant pro who sold you the square-head hybrid for $550 when it should have cost $119. Go in the shop with this putter when there's nobody around, and pop-pop-pop."

"Excuse me," I said. "Are we talking about actually shooting people?"

The Putter Man said, "No, my man, we're not. For the good of golf, we're talkin' about killin' people that ought to be kilt."

Holding on to my posters, I scurried out of the merchandise hall as quickly as possible without knocking anyone down.

THE NEW WORLD TOUR

The PGA of America has announced that it is entertaining the idea of taking its PGA Championship, one of the year's four majors, to countries outside the United States.

—NEWS ITEM

AM PLEASED TO greet you today as the commissioner of the Global Tour of Professional Golf, or the GTPG, which is how my staff is already referring to it. Their pronunciation seems to have settled on "Gitpig." That may have legs.

This is a great time for me to speak to you in light of the recent announcement from the PGA of America about taking its major to foreign lands.

Such a move is bound to have volcanic eruptions within our sport. Rest assured, however, that no ruling body of the game is going to beat us to Istanbul, Budapest, Hamburg, Beirut, or any other desirable area.

Many of you remember me from the days when I was the managing director of Cruise Golf, the company I rescued financially after the Princess of the Fairways was lost off the coast of Java due to overcrowding.

Others among you may recall I was once the editor in

chief of *Vacation Golf,* the publication in which I came up with the successful ad campaign "Leave the Kids at Home If They Know How to Feed Themselves."

Before I continue, let me publicly thank the people who selected me for this prestigious position. I refer to the leaders of our PGA Tour, the European Tour, the Asian Tour, the Japan Golf Tour, the Sunshine Tour—that's in South Africa—and the PGA Tour of Australasia.

Oh, and the Tour de las Americas, which, quite frankly, I didn't know existed until a day ago.

I found out about it when I received an email wishing me luck in the new job. It came from an American tournament sponsor in Mexico City who was only hours away from facing a firing squad. It had something to do with missing funds.

All he had done, he assured me, was make the casual remark that Emiliano Zapata would have lived longer if he had devoted his life to golf instead of raiding villages.

That aside, I want to fill you in on some of the promising tournaments I'm hoping to see launched. My basic plan is to remain global but take the Tour to more familiar places around the world.

I'm known for my slogans, as you are aware. A few I've come up with might give you a hint of the directions our tour will be taking. One: "Let the pygmies keep New Guinea." Two: "Malaysia is for *National Geographic.*" Three: "If you order the paella in Spain, make sure to find out how much in it is dead and how much is still alive."

As I said, I'm going to stick to major cities for tournament sites. No more of this Johor Open in Bahru foolishness. I mean, who knew about *that one* other than some birds and insects?

Already under way is a unique tournament we're calling the Socialist Paradise Invitational in Buenos Aires. We would like to have the support of the Argentine president, and we're in the process of finding out if Argentina has a current president.

Some lady is reported to hold the office, but my people haven't been able to grab her for a statement. I'm told we had her pinned down at a jewelry counter in Saks Fifth Avenue in New York City a week ago, but she slipped away. We now hear she may be browsing around Harrods in London.

A government official has given us guidelines for the event. The field must be limited to fifty pros who have never won a tournament of any kind and hate the capitalistic societies into which they were born. All fifty will be declared winners and given equal prize money and identical trophies.

We do need the approval of the Argentine president, or at least a statement from one of her assistants carrying the shopping bags.

While in that part of the world, we would follow up with a tournament in Bogotá, Colombia. We're tentatively calling it the Coca Leaf Classic. It would be played at The Country Club of Raul's Cartel. We hear it's a challenging course that winds through groves of coca trees and processing plants that were uncovered by the DEA.

To attract a good field we're thinking the winner should receive $2 million in prize money along with a squad of armed guards to see him to the airport, plus a fighter escort to accompany his Avianca flight out of the country.

The Middle East holds some promise for us. I can't imagine anyone not getting excited over a tournament I'm calling The Fracas in Damascus.

I say a truce could be put in place for a week in the capital city of Syria, and top pros from various tours could compete with golfing members of al-Qaeda, ISIS, and the Syrian army. Apart from the competition, it would be GTPG's effort in advancing the cause of peace in the region.

Not to ignore the USA. I have a team event in mind. The Immigration. It has that one-word ring to it. Like the Masters, the Players, the Tradition.

I envision forty four-man teams battling it out over 72 holes on one of the three thousand courses we can choose from in Scottsdale. A team would consist of a name pro, an illegal alien, a border guard, and a member of the United States Senate. First prize for the winning team would be Yuma, Arizona. Second prize, Nogales.

I can't tell you how proud I am to be a part of golf's explosion.

So I will close with this statement. The torch has been passed to a new organization. Let the word go forth from this time and this place to the PGA of America—Mogadishu is ours!

JUNIOR GOLF

Yesterday's Junior Golfer

Billy Bob rises, gets dressed, makes his bed, goes to breakfast, talks sports and news of the day with mom and dad. Asks if it's okay if he plays a round of golf after school today at Dirt Track Muny.

Billy Bob's dad says, "Sure, son. But keep your head down, swing slowly." With a smile, mom says, "Fairways and greens, sweetheart." Billy Bob gives mom a kiss, dad a hug, leaves.

Billy Bob goes to school. Learns that America is beautiful, the hope of the world. Hears several foreign countries don't speak English, don't like cheeseburgers, and could be trouble in the future. Teacher says America may have to teach them a thing or two someday.

Billy Bob rides his bike to Dirt Track Muny, his canvas bag of golf clubs strapped over his shoulder. Billy Bob sweeps out pro shop, unloads boxes, helps head pro do other chores. Head pro says Billy Bob is good kid, lets him play for free today.

Billy Bob plays 18 with a postman, a mechanic, and a truck driver.

Billy Bob shoots even-par 72, his best score ever at Dirt Track. Postman, mechanic, and truck driver each lose a quarter to Billy Bob. He believes this is the best day of his life.

Billy Bob rides his bike to girlfriend's house, takes her through his round. Tells her about his birdies at 1, 7, and 14, and the unlucky bogeys at 5, 10, and 13. He describes in detail the long chip shot that saves his par at 15. His girlfriend, Patricia Mary Alice, seems excited to hear all this.

Billy Bob and Patricia Mary Alice play records and dance in her living room. Their favorite songs are "The Old Piano Roll Blues" and "Walkin' My Baby Back Home."

Billy Bob thinks he may be in love. Kisses Patricia Mary Alice and goes home for a good night's sleep so he can wake up fresh tomorrow, mow the lawn, run errands for mom, and tackle Dirt Track Muny again.

Today's Junior Golfer

Ricky Sean rises in his bedroom suite of family's 35,000-square-foot home. Selects new golf shirt he will wear only once. Goes downstairs for breakfast. Finds dad sitting at breakfast table, talking on cell, firing people.

Ricky Sean sneers at yolk broken on egg and bread not toasted properly, gives mother holy hell. Mother begs forgiveness. Ricky Sean shrugs, tells mother to go clean a room, sweep a floor, whatever.

Ricky Sean cranks up his bright blue Maserati, impatiently plows through slow-rising garage door. Says garage door is stupid. Dad should have it fixed.

Ricky Sean speeds through city, causes city bus to turn over, injuring twenty-six people. Ricky Sean cusses city bus for hogging road. Ricky Sean fazes school today. School is boring. All teachers do is talk about things.

Ricky Sean cruises to Nasdaq Country Club, eases Maserati into handicap parking space near entrance. So-called music blares from Maserati's stereo. The Transgender Vampires are performing "Tattooed Skinny People."

Ricky Sean is told by valet parker he can't stay in handicap space. Ricky Sean says he can because he is handicapped. Valet parker asks how he's handicapped. Ricky Sean says, "I'm hitting a hot pull. Gotta work on it." Valet parker says okay, leave car here, accepts $100 bill from Ricky Sean.

Ricky Sean goes to practice range, removes clubs from golf bag made of white rhino leather. Club member strolls over, admires clubs, asks what model they are. Ricky Sean says, "Weapons of mass destruction. They cost more than your neighborhood. Get away from me, old fool."

Ricky Sean hits practice balls. Turns hot pull into crop-duster cut. Turns crop-duster cut into flame-out sky dive. Turns flame-out sky dive into freeway divider. Goes back to hot pull. Works hot pull into Javelin rocket launch.

Ricky Sean joins game with three low-handicap club members. Shoots 62, wins $8,000. Members insist on emergency nine. Ricky Sean fires a 31, wins $16,000 more.

Ricky Sean picks up girlfriend, Ashley Amber. They dine at In-N-Out Caviar, go to Movie Tomb, drink champagne, watch *Flesh Eating Swamp Fiends.* Ricky Sean drives to lake with Ashley Amber, parks. They listen to so-called music on car stereo. Ricky Sean says his favorite rock group is Bleeding Scabs. Ashley Amber says her favorite rock group is Loudmouth Sluts. They argue. Ricky Sean says he's too tired for sex. Dumps Ashley Amber at after-hours club, goes home.

At home Ricky Sean discovers college acceptance letters waiting for him from Stanford, Duke, Yale, Harvard, Northwestern, and Notre Dame. Ricky Sean decides to skip college, go straight to PGA Tour. Won't have to talk about things.

Q-AND-A WITH SERGIO

THE AUTHOR OF *Sometimes It Goes In* and *Me, Sergio* has been a star in the sport of golf for more than fifteen years. Has he met his own expectations as a writer and a golfer? What does the future hold for him?

What are you currently reading?

I have just finished *Mr. Tiger Goes Wild*. They tricked me. It was not about golf. Now I plan to start on *Winnie-the-Pooh*. I have always been interested in Churchill and what he meant to the world. If Churchill had not won the war, there would not be a European Tour. This is true, yes? Not to speak badly about Germans. I have many German friends through golf. I like their schnitzel.

Do you prefer to read old books or new books?

No book is old if you have not read it. That is a dumb question.

How often do you reread a book?

The hardest book I ever tried to reread was *The Little*

Mouse, the Red Ripe Strawberry, and the Big Hungry Bear.
When I got through the title I was too tired to go on. But I
was not tricked this time. I asked if the book was about golf,
and when they laughed, I put it back on the shelf. I should
have known Jack Nicklaus would choose a shorter title.

*What is the most important thing you have learned about
the game of golf since you wrote* Sometimes It Goes In, *your
instruction book?*

I should have included a chapter on how to talk to the golf
ball. For too many years I made the mistake of standing up
to a drive and at the moment of impact yelling, *"Vámonos!"* I
have learned this is not the way. It is better to whisper, *"Qué
estupendo."*

The greatest players did not need to know this. The golf
ball knew who held the club. When Jack Nicklaus hit the
ball, the ball knew not to go crooked into the sea, where it
would live until a shark ate it like a peanut. The ball knew
not to soar into the forest, where it would lead a lonely life
until the brown bear found himself an hors d'oeuvre.

It is an amazing thing. Today the golf ball is a rock and
goes straight no matter who swings at it, except for me, Sergio. For me, it looks for sand, weeds, water, wind. This is a
curiosity, is it not?

*What golf books would you be embarrassed not to have
read yet?*

First I would say Ben Hogan's *Nine Lessons, the Modern
Funerals of Golf.* I hear Hogan would tell me to pronate. But I
am already a pro, so this information would be useless to me.

They say Bobby Jones wrote good books, but he played
with hickory. Wood is for cooking or nailing a plank.

I started to read Tommy Armour's classic, *How to Play Your Best Golf All the Time*, but the title put me off. It is impossible, what he says to do. Golf does not allow this, except for Tiger Woods, who acts like he has played the best golf even when he suffers back spasms. I can hear him whine from here.

Let's talk about your autobiography.

My what?

Your new book, Me, Sergio. *It is aptly named.*

It wasn't named by anybody but me. Some of my friends wanted to call it *El Niño*, but that is something the press made up. I am not a storm or an ocean or a weatherman. I am a human, like almost everybody else.

What is the most important thing you would like someone to take away from your book?

I would like for the person to take away the whole book and leave $26.95 on the table. I am making a joke here. You should write it down. It is funnier than anything Tiger Woods ever said.

What does the book say about you that we may not know?

My book proves in detail that I am a greater player than people realize. I have won many tournaments in Europe, the United States, South Africa, Asia, and some country I can't pronounce. It was down near Malaysia or someplace. I am also a Ryder Cup hero. Why do Ryder Cups not count as majors? It is a good question, yes?

I have finished in a lot of top fives in the majors. I would have won three or four if enough people had lost. But they didn't. It was a cruel thing.

I was this close three times, but my putt missed and

someone else's putt went in. How do you explain this? I have beaten my head against the wall thinking about it, but not so hard as to hurt myself. A golfer needs to be careful that the wall is not made of brick.

But time is on my side. I am only thirty-five. I have many future majors to win or lose. And in the meantime, I am a celebrity who is called by only one name, me, Sergio. Like Madonna.

MASTERS MEMORIES

ARITHMETIC TELLS ME I've covered sixty-four consecutive Masters tournaments through 2014. By any stretch of the imagination that's a lot of peach cobbler in the clubhouse. Oh, and golf.

The streak started in 1951 when I was a college sophomore but was also working for a daily newspaper in Fort Worth, and I was mainly in Augusta to cover the exploits of a contestant from the hometown. Guy named Ben Hogan.

Best Parking Spot
Mine. The one that Chairman Billy Payne awarded me in 2010. It's only a few steps from the media center marked: CHAIRMAN RESERVED. He and I agreed that I'd earned it.

Best Street
Magnolia Lane, the heavily shaded main entrance to the clubhouse. No sharp turns toward Appomattox, happily.

Best Traditions
Ceremonial tee shots.
Including amateurs in the field.
Bringing back the past greats.
Keeping the big veranda trees on life support.

Welcome Reversals
Switching the nines in '35.
Adding lady members in 2012.
Contestants getting rid of their seventies bell-bottom
   slacks.

Nice Strokes by Chairmen
Cliff Roberts. Made the Masters what it is.
Hord Hardin. Had the bent greens installed.
Hootie Johnson. Stood up to the media heat. Refused
   to be intimidated by howling ladies and other
   protesters.
Billy Payne. Brought in Condi Rice and Darla Moore.

Handy Improvements
Cumulative scoring system.
Pressroom changed from tent to Quonset hut.
Pressroom changed from Quonset hut to auditorium.
New tee on 18.
Seeing Augusta, Georgia, evolve from a strip club,
   tattoo parlor, army town with only one good
   restaurant, the Town Tavern, into a lively city that
   retains the scenery and charm of the genteel Old
   South.

Fiercest Hazards
Rae's Creek on the 12th.
The water in front of 15.
The water left of the 11th green.
The trees right of the 18th fairway.
The tributary of Rae's Creek as it idles left of the
    fairway and in front of the green at 13.
Tommy Bolt in the old days—after a bad round.

A Quote That Lives On
Seve Ballesteros explaining how he four-putted one of the
lightning-fast greens: "I miss . . . I miss . . . I miss . . . I make."

Top Quip
Dave Marr to Arnold Palmer on the 72nd tee in 1964 when
Arnold was leading by six and Dave was holding on to second. When Arnold asked Dave if there was anything he
could do to help him here, Marr said, "Make a 12."

Best Players Who Never Won Masters
Ernie Els, Ken Venturi, Lloyd Mangrum, Julius Boros, Gene
Littler, Greg Norman, Tom Weiskopf, Johnny Miller, Cur-
tis Strange, Lanny Wadkins, Lee Trevino, Tommy Bolt,
Hale Irwin, Lawson Little.

Memorable Shots
Arnold Palmer stiffing an eight-iron at number 12
    for a birdie in 1962. It put him in command
    of the playoff with Gary Player and Dow
    Finsterwald.

Jack Nicklaus's monster one-iron onto the 15th green
in 1975 in the heat of the final-round battle with
Johnny Miller and Tom Weiskopf. Jack gave the
shot the description it deserved: "Greatest pressure
shot of my life."

Phil Mickelson's six-iron second out of the trees,
through an opening the size of a keyhole, and onto
the green for a birdie that sent him to his win in
2010.

Tiger Woods's chip-in birdie in 2005 from in back
of the 16th green. It starts toward downtown,
changes its mind, returns, and slowly creeps
down a slope and into the cup.

Amateur Billy Joe Patton's hole in one at number 6 in
1954. It came in the last round and for a while gave
him the lead over Snead and Hogan, and caused
the loudest Southern whoop since the discovery of
sweet-potato pie.

Memorable Putts

Jack Nicklaus's 40-footer for a birdie on 16 in 1975 to
hold off Miller and Weiskopf, followed by the leap
that left "Bear tracks."

Jackie Burke's 40-footer—it seemed longer—all
the way across the 17th green in 1956 to overtake
Ken Venturi.

Ben Crenshaw's creeping, crawling 60-footer for
birdie on number 10 in the last round that paved
the way for his first Masters jacket in 1984.

Ben Hogan's downhill 25-footer for birdie on 18 in
  1967 to complete a back-nine 30 and a round of
  six-under 66—at the age of fifty-five.
Tom Watson's 20-foot birdie on 17 of the final round
  in 1977 that gave him the Masters over Nicklaus
  and served as a prelude to their monumental duel
  in the British Open at Turnberry in July.
Phil Mickelson's wobbly 20-footer in 2004 that
  barely toppled into the cup on the 72nd green to
  give him the win by a stroke as Ernie Els, "the
  leader in the clubhouse," looked on.

Free Drop, Anyone?

Arnold Palmer invoking the embedded-ball rule at the
  12th hole in 1958, turning a 5 into a 3, which won
  him the Masters over Ken Venturi, who grieved
  over it the rest of his career.
Ernie Els out of the deep, dense forest on number
  11 in 2004—a peculiar ruling at best—which
  could have been The Drop That Won the Masters,
  except Phil Mickelson overcame it.

A Horror Film in the Making

Greg Norman's meltdown on Sunday in 1996. He gradually
and painfully turned a six-stroke lead into a losing 78.

Moments for Name-Dropping

The wife and I having dinner in the clubhouse with
  chairman Clifford Roberts, at his invitation.

Lunching with Bobby Jones in the Jones Cabin with
Charley Price, fellow writer, who knew Jones well
and got me invited. I wanted to talk about Bobby
Jones and Bobby Jones wanted to talk about Ben
Hogan.

Meeting Alistair Cooke and having lunch with him
on the clubhouse balcony. Herb Wind introduced
him to me as "Al Cooke."

Meeting the Duke of Windsor on the veranda, only
because Fred Corcoran insisted on introducing me.

Meeting and having lunch with the actress Joan
Fontaine in the Trophy Room, and keeping her
company while her husband at the time, Alfred
Wright, my *Sports Illustrated* colleague, went off to
talk to golfers.

The Ten Best Masters I Have Covered

1953 Ben Hogan breaks the 72-hole record by going
14 under, starts the Triple Crown journey. Calls it
"the best four-day stretch of golf I've ever played."
And it was on those scratchy old rye greens that
seemed so fast back in the day.

1954 Sam Snead wins a historic playoff over Hogan,
70 to 71, basically on a long chip-in for birdie
at the 10th hole. Prior to the playoff, the week
belonged to amateur Billy Joe Patton, who alter-
nately won it and lost it with his brazen style.

1956 Amateur Ken Venturi opens with a 66 and
leads for seventy straight holes, looking like a lock
to become the first amateur to win a major since

Johnny Goodman in the U.S. Open of 1933. But
on a day of furiously strong winds, he slow-bleeds
to an 80, and Jackie Burke nips him by a stroke.

1960 Arnold Palmer birdies the last two holes to
edge Ken Venturi and win his second Masters
and become the new big star the game had been
waiting for.

1975 Jack Nicklaus plays his grittiest pressure golf to
hold off Johnny Miller and Tom Weiskopf to grab
his fifth Masters.

1980 Seve Ballesteros gives birth to European golf.
And Seve-style golf. He takes a ten-stroke lead
into the final nine and plays them by way of
Savannah, Milledgeville, and Atlanta, but hangs
on for a four-stroke win.

1986 Not a dry eye in the house or all of outdoors
as a forty-six-year-old Jack Nicklaus returns
from wherever he's been to fire a 65 on Sunday
and knock off Seve Ballesteros, Greg Norman,
and Tom Kite to win his record sixth Masters and
eighteenth pro major.

1995 Sentiment wins the Masters. Rather it's Ben
Crenshaw taking his second green jacket with
what he calls "a fifteenth club in my bag." Which
meant the inspiration of Harvey Penick, his
lifelong teacher and friend, who had passed away
two weeks earlier.

1997 Records tumble in every direction as a twenty-
one-year-old Tiger Woods gives the golf world
a dominating figure it hasn't seen since Jack

Nicklaus. In setting a new record of 18-under 270,
he doesn't three-putt a single green in 72 holes,
which of course on the Augusta National greens
is against the law. It was the start of something
big that would only get bigger.

2004 Phil Mickelson finally wins a major, and does
it in dramatic fashion. Well, it had taken him long
enough. He'd been expected to do it since he was
born, if not before.

Best Typing (Me Division)

1951 "Ben Hogan played it safe this time at 18 to
avoid the three-putt that had cost him the '46
Masters. He laid up for a chip shot. How often do
you see a great golfer miss a green intentionally?"

1961 "Gary Player is the Masters champion today
because Arnold Palmer was in too big of a hurry
to win it. The way Palmer butchered the last hole
for a double-bogey 6, it might as well have been a
slab of meat."

1986 "A strange object slowly bled to death before
our very eyes for four hours, and it wasn't even
a shark. What Greg Norman did to himself was
unleash every Great White Can of Tuna joke in
the book."

1995 "Not to bury the lead, but Ben Crenshaw
winning this Masters for the late Harvey Penick
made it, all in all, a very bad week for atheists."

2009 "When Angel Cabrera wound up winning
the greatly anticipated 2009 Masters, it was like

going to a Broadway hit and finding out that the
star, Tiger Woods, was off that night, and his
replacement was the cabdriver who dropped you
off at the theater."

2010 "Tiger Woods saved a lot of guys a lot of
money. If he'd won this Masters, five million golfers would have gone into sex rehab."

Longest Tee Shot That Should Have Placed Bubba Watson Under Arrest

His 366-yard drive on number 13 in the final round of the
2014 Masters turned the dangerous par-5 into a sissy and
said good-bye to Jordan Spieth.

Favorite Monuments

Hogan Bridge at 12.

Nelson Bridge at 13.

Sarazen Bridge at 15.

Me. After covering my sixty-fourth Masters in a row.

U.S. OPEN MEMORIES

SIXTY-ONE IS A lot of U.S. Opens and a lot of pressure—and I'm just talking about the deadlines. In any case, I invite you to de-anchor yourself and your putter and come along with me as I dredge up memories and thoughts from covering our national championship over seven decades.

Best Question
Jack Nicklaus to the USGA's P. J. Boatwright in the 1972 Open at Pebble Beach: "What did you do with all the grass?"

Biggest Distraction
At Oakmont in 1994, Ernie Els was halfway toward winning his first U.S. Open while the rest of us were watching the O.J. Bronco chase.

Best First Tee, Best Flagsticks, Best Quarry Holes
Merion, Merion, and Merion.

First Golfer to Choose Winning the Open over Death by Dehydration
Ken Venturi at Congressional in 1964. They opened the coffin and out he crawled to shoot 66-70 the last day.

Best Open
Hard to go up against Palmer, Hogan, and Nicklaus battling down the stretch at Cherry Hills in 1960.

Second-Best Open
Hogan bringing the monster to its knees with that final-round 67 at Oakland Hills in 1951.

Dullest Open
No contest. The Germanater, Martin Kaymer, winning by eight at Pinehurst in 2014. Those turtleback greens sucked the life out of everything, including the press tent.

Greatest Streak
Ben Hogan finished in the top ten in sixteen straight Opens, winning five. Yeah, I count the wartime Open in '42. So did he. How often do I have to say this?

Most Surprising Winner of Two Opens
Andy North at Cherry Hills in 1978 and at Oakland Hills in 1985. "It was an awful Open," Andy said in '85. "Jack didn't win."

When Did Mesopotamia Get the Open?
The clubhouse at Medinah still looks like the Babylon Marriott.

My Favorite Courses That Have Never Held the Open (and Can't, Won't, or Never Will)
Pine Valley, Cypress Point, Seminole, National Golf Links, Bel-Air, Brook Hollow, San Francisco Golf, Maidstone, Winged Foot East, Shady Oaks, Black Diamond Ranch.

Scariest Spectator
In the gallery at Oakland Hills in 1996 was Jack Kevorkian, "Dr. Death."

Funniest Thing "Dr. Death" Said
"I'm going to walk up to Jack Nicklaus and tell him, 'If you don't win, I'm here.'"

First Cross-Handed Putting Grip to Win Open
Old Sarge, Orville Moody, used it at Champions in 1969. It was considered rare in golf for many years, but then the world went nutso-whacko with bellies and broomsticks and claws and claw threes and reverse retards.

Best Quotes
Jackie Burke on USGA officials: "Most of them don't know the rules. They just want to play blue coat and arm band."

Cary Middlecoff, after winning the Open at Oak Hill in 1956 while sitting in the clubhouse, which was after he sat in the clubhouse at Medinah in 1949 and won the Open: "Nobody wins the Open. It wins you."

Tom Weiskopf, laughing after hearing about Johnny Miller's 63 at Oakmont in 1973: "I didn't know Miller made the cut!"

Tommy Bolt at Southern Hills in 1958 after accusing a writer from the *Tulsa World* of printing his age as forty-nine and hearing the writer say it was a typographical error: "Typographical error, my ass—it was a perfect four and a perfect nine."

Lee Trevino after winning at Oak Hill in 1968 and being asked what he was going to do with all the prize money: "Buy the Alamo and give it back to the Mexicans."

Joe Dey, the USGA's executive director, when hearing complaints about the punishing, unfair setup of Oakland Hills in 1951: "You play the course the way you find it."

Name the Player Who Has Won All of His Opens on Public Courses
Tiger Woods. At Pebble Beach, Bethpage, Torrey Pines.

Greatest Players Who Never Won the Open
Sam Snead, Phil Mickelson, Jimmy Demaret, Seve Ballesteros, Greg Norman, Macdonald Smith, Nick Faldo, Tom Weiskopf, Ben Crenshaw, Lanny Wadkins, Henry Picard, Paul Runyan, Harry Cooper, Horton Smith, Denny Shute, Bobby Locke, Henry Cotton, Jackie Burke.

Best Finishing Hole
The 18th at Winged Foot. It's not exactly calendar art, but this par-4 has made things happen: Bobby Jones's 12-foot putt to tie Al Espinosa in 1929, Billy Casper's clutch putts

for pars in 1959, Hale Irwin's two-iron shot in 1974, Fuzzy Zoeller's white towel waving at Greg Norman in 1984, and Phil Mickelson's mind-boggling gift to Geoff Ogilvy in 2006. One way or another, it's a finishing hole that's had something to say about the winner of every Open at Winged Foot.

Worst Finishing Hole
It's understandable why no one has written a poem about Lucas Glover playing Bethpage Black's par-4 18th with a six-iron and a nine-iron in 2009. It wasn't exactly Hogan at Merion.

The Trouble with Pebble's 17th
Take away two shots—Nicklaus's one-iron stiff in 1972 and Tom Watson's holed-out chip in 1982—and what have you got? A par-3 hole that's long, hard, and dull.

Last Dress Shirt and Necktie to Win Open
Ralph Guldahl's attire when he won at Oakland Hills in 1937, and again at Cherry Hills in 1938.

Clubhouse That Looks the Most Haunted
Baltusrol in Springfield, New Jersey.

Clubhouse That Looks Most Like a Mansion Where I'd Like to Live
Winged Foot in Westchester County.

Clubhouse That Looks Least Like a Place Where You Would Hold an Open
Champions, which is almost near Houston.

Fastest Greens
Merion, Oakmont, Oakland Hills, Winged Foot. Jack Nicklaus might as well have been talking about the four of them when he said of Winged Foot in '74, "It's like playing miniature golf without sideboards."

Best (or Worst) Rough
Toss-up. Olympic in 1955, where it was damp, clinging, and creeping up the calves. Oakland Hills in 1951, where Sam Snead said, "These fairways are so narrow, you have to walk sideways to keep the rough from snagging your pants."

Even the Greatest Can Give Them Away
1928 Bobby Jones held a five-shot lead going into the final 18 at Olympia Fields but stumbled to a six-over 77, allowing Johnny Farrell to tie him. "I finished like a yellow dog," said Jones. Farrell won the 36-hole playoff by one stroke.

1939 Sam Snead's famous 8 on the last hole of the Spring Mill course at Philadelphia Country Club. A par 5 would have won, a bogey 6 would have tied, but Sam thought he needed a birdie. He drove wildly into deep rough, took four more to get out of weeds and sand to reach the green, then three-putted.

1946 Byron Nelson suffered a penalty stroke in the morning 18 at Canterbury when his caddie accidentally moved his ball while stepping under the ropes, yet he still had a two-stroke lead on the field in the afternoon with only two holes to

play. Uncharacteristically, he bogeyed both with
a three-putt and a poor chip, and ultimately lost
a 36-hole playoff by a shot to Lloyd Mangrum.
Afterward in a radio interview with Bill Stern,
whose show was sponsored by a razor-blade company, Byron said, "Bill, if you'll just give me one of
those things you're advertising, I'll cut my throat."

1966 Arnold Palmer in the last round at Olympic
held a seven-stroke lead over Billy Casper with
only nine to play, but he somehow frittered all of
them away, and then had to make a clutch putt
on 18 to tie. In the playoff, Arnold blew a three-
shot lead, but this Open was destined to belong to
Casper.

Best Shots

1950 Hogan's two-iron from 189 yards to the 18th
at Merion to secure a par and a tie with Lloyd
Mangrum and George Fazio, and put himself
on track to complete the All-Time Comeback in
Sports History.

1958 Tommy Bolt's 200-yard, uphill four-wood to
the last green at Southern Hills for an easy two-
putt par, permitting him to dodge one last chance
to explode. "Ain't this something?" I heard him
say as I was walking with him inside the ropes. "I
done Ben Hogan-ed it. Old Tom is gonna win his-
self a U.S. of Open."

1960 Arnold Palmer's 346-yard drive onto the 1st
green at Cherry Hills, the shot that propelled him

to his historic 65. Fifty years later I asked Arnold
if the hole would be a par-5 for him now. He said,
"No, but it would be three shots."

1972 Jack Nicklaus's one-iron from 218 yards to two
inches of the cup at Pebble Beach's par-3 17th hole.

1976 Jerry Pate's five-iron second shot out of the
rough and over the water to within two feet of
the flag on the last hole to win at Atlanta Athletic
Club. His reaction: "How 'bout that, sports fans?"

1982 Tom Watson's chip-in for a birdie at Pebble
Beach's par-3 17th to hold off Jack Nicklaus.

Most Stunning Putts

1951 Hogan's 18-footer for birdie on the last green
at Oakland Hills for his shocking 67 that brought
"the monster" to his, her, or its knees.

1983 Larry Nelson's 60-footer at Oakmont's 16th
on the weather-delayed Monday. The putt went in
for a birdie and sank Tom Watson with it.

1990 Hale Irwin's 45-foot birdie on the 72nd
green—and his victory lap that followed. It gave
him a tie with Mike Donald, whom he would
beat in the playoff.

Best Parking Spot

The one I had for more than forty years next to the
clubhouse before the USGA took it away from me
and gave it to some corporate slug who would only
be there for the shrimp puffs in a hospitality tent.

BRITISH OPEN MEMORIES

AT ALL THE forty-six British Opens I've covered, it's mostly been about seeking out a good serving of fish and chips, which is usually the one where the fish tastes like chips and the chips taste like fish. But let's move on.

Best Oddity
Harry Vardon won six British Opens, but never at St. Andrews. Tom Watson won five British Opens, but never at St. Andrews. Walter Hagen won four British Opens, but never at St. Andrews. And John Daly won at St. Andrews?

Favorite Open Course Other Than St. Andrews
Carnoustie. The name derives from two words: *carn*, which was the first bubble-head shepherd's crook, and *noustie*, a soup consisting of sheep's blood and minced gutta-perchas.

But If You Want to Have Fun Playing Golf in Scotland
Skip most of today's Open courses. Go to North Berwick, Crail, Gullane, Dunbar, Prestwick. Blends good golf with magic scenery and Old World charm.

First Memory of Playing the Old Course
I was doing pretty well until I got to number 12. That's where my caddie said, "Aye, now comes the golf course."

Best Par-4 (and Par-5)
The Road Hole at St. Andrews.

Funniest Thing Anybody Ever Said about St. Andrews
Sam Snead, while winning the Open on the Old Course in '46: "It looks like there used to be a golf course here."

Nicest Thing Ben Hogan Said about Carnoustie
After winning the Open there in '53: "I'll try to remember to send you people some lawn mowers."

The Descriptive Jerry Pate
Blending three sports into one, Pate said to Ben Crenshaw before the last round at Royal Lytham & St. Annes in 1979: "Gentle, you're my pick tomorrow. I believe you can rope-a-dope that old hook of yours right into victory lane."

Best Request
Jack Nicklaus's mom to a security guard who asked why she should be allowed into the grandstand behind the 18th

green at St. Andrews in 1978: "My son is about to win the Open, and I would like to watch it."

The Story Everyone Was Poised to Write, but . . .
At fifty-nine years of age, the incredible Tom Watson missed an 8-foot putt to win the 2009 Open at Turnberry, which would have been his sixth. He then lost the playoff to Stewart Cink. I've been to funerals more uplifting.

Best Decade for the Claret Jug
The 1970s. Winners were Jack Nicklaus ('70 and '78), Lee Trevino ('71 and '72), Tom Weiskopf ('73), Gary Player ('74), Tom Watson ('75 and '77), Johnny Miller ('76), and Seve Ballesteros ('79). Not a lurker in the bunch.

Favorite Tabloid Headline
Seen during '92 Open at Muirfield: "Robin Hood's Body Found in Sherwood Forest: Died Clutching Maid Marian's Knickers."

Beverage Critique
Lee Trevino having a lukewarm lager at Muirfield in 1972: "No wonder everybody over here is so wrinkled up."

Best Advice, Mother Division
Adam Scott's mother, a former club champion in Australia, to her son: "It's all about the putting, Adam."

Ranking the Rota
Number of Opens I covered by venue: St. Andrews (Old Course), eight; Muirfield, Birkdale, Lytham, Troon, six each; Sandwich (Royal St. Georges), five; Turnberry, four; Carnoustie, three; and Hoylake (Royal Liverpool), one. Favorites for combined course design, housing, village food, proximity to club: 1. Old Course, 2. Muirfield, 3. Hoylake, 4. Carnoustie, 5. Lytham, 6. Birkdale, 7. Troon, 8. Turnberry, 9. Sandwich.

A Response to Criticism
At wind-chilled and stormy Lytham in 1979, a competitor complained to R&A secretary Keith Mackenzie that the course was impossible and something ought to be done about it. "Well, we can't shut it down," Mackenzie said. "The members would only want to go out and play."

What Is That Out There?
The Ailsa Craig. A bird sanctuary in the Firth of Clyde at Turnberry. It looks like the world's largest half-sunken football, or Governor Christie.

But the Owner Promised Four
Our rented house at Birkdale in '91 had one bathroom for eight guys.

Days of His Life
Rod Pampling led the first round of the 1999 Open at Carnoustie with a 71. But he shot a second-round 86 and missed

the cut. We might have expected it from a guy whose name sounded like a British coin.

When You Have Time on Your Hands

Dave Marr's 70 in the first round at Muirfield in 1972 was only one shot back of the leader, Tony Jacklin. He was invited to the pressroom for an interview. Since his tee time for the second round was not until four thirty the next afternoon, he was asked how he would spend all that time. Marr said, "Oh, I'll tour Edinburgh Castle, do a little shopping, probably take in a movie."

Best Hole in One

Gene Sarazen, then seventy-one, aced the Postage Stamp at Troon with a five-iron in 1973, and received a wire of congratulations from Howard Hughes. In the second round, Sarazen holed out from a bunker on the same hole—the 123-yard 8th—for a birdie. So the geezer in plus-fours played the hole in three under par and never had to putt.

Best Player Who Never Won the Open

Byron Nelson. But he entered only twice. He was fifth at Carnoustie in 1937 on a trip that primarily involved the Ryder Cup, and he finished T-32 at St. Andrews in 1955. Which happened to be the journey where he won the French Open at La Boulie near Paris. This was Byron's last pro victory, coming nine years after he'd retired—and the best he could do was shoot 271, a mere 17 under par.

Sometimes Rules Are Quite Stupid

In 2003 at Sandwich, Mark Roe and Jesper Parnevik forgot to exchange scorecards on the first tee and didn't realize it until it was too late. Therefore, they signed for the wrong score and were disqualified. It was hard to believe that the officials didn't know that Roe had shot the 67 and Parnevik had shot the 81. But rules are rules, the R&A said. One could only wonder if rules would have been rules if this had happened to Tiger Woods.

You Don't Skip a Major

Curtis Strange did in 1985. He skipped Sandwich. Earlier in the year he had refused to lay up in front of the creek at 13 and blew the Masters. This time he laid up short of the Atlantic Ocean.

These Darn Inconveniences

A contestant named Richard Boxall was challenging for the lead in the third round at Birkdale in 1991 when he collapsed after hitting his tee shot at the 9th hole. Broken leg. Colin Montgomerie, in the same pairing, played on, and later said, "I was totally devastated. My concentration went completely." So, Colin. Let me see if I understand this. Your eventual tie for twenty-sixth was the guy's fault for breaking his leg?

As Nicknames Go

When Ernie Els punished the press by losing the playoff to a total unknown, Todd Hamilton, at Troon in 2004, he earned a new nickname. The Big Queasy. But the likable and cooperative Ernie has made up for it since. Like winning at Lytham in 2012. And it's not to be forgotten that Els has two U.S. Opens and two British Opens in the bank.

Breaking the Code

Nick Faldo had been mentioning "code name Basil" in regard to some secret improvement in his game, but he didn't reveal the secret until his win at Muirfield in 1992. Basil referred to a hand puppet called Basil Brush, which used to appear on British TV. David Leadbetter, Faldo's instructor, told him to think of brushing the top of the grass with his putter through impact, but the putterhead must accelerate through the stroke. Only Basil to win an Open.

When Honesty Prevailed

Greg Norman, after losing the four-hole playoff at Troon in 1989 although he'd birdied the first two holes, was asked whether destiny owed him one. His response: "It [expletive deleted] owes me about four."

They Do Good Streakers

Peter Jacobsen took one down—a guy—at Sandwich in 1985, and explained later, "You have to square up like a linebacker, but right before impact, make sure you turn your head." It was a sixteen-year-old girl named Sherrie Bevan at Birkdale in 1991 who shed her togs and gave José María Olazábal a kiss as he strode down the first fairway. "I don't know what got into her," Sherrie's mother said. "I looked around, and she was out of it."

Worst Speech

At the annual British Golf Writers dinner in St. Andrews before the 2010 Open got under way, Prince Andrew was the featured speaker. Everybody was excited, right up until he spoke. And spoke. And spoke. To say the speech was dreary and uninformative would not be accurate enough. When it finally ended, Alastair Johnston, the Scotsman who for years at IMG looked after Arnold Palmer and Gary Player, and who was seated at our table—the *Golf Digest* table—said, "Now I remember why I wanted to immigrate to the United States."

Best Open I Covered

Almost too many to choose from, typewriter-wise. The Watson-Nicklaus duel at Turnberry in '77. Trevino, Nicklaus, and Jacklin fighting it out at Muirfied in '72. Palmer trouncing Troon in '62. Mickelson's marvelous finish at Muirfield in 2013. But I'll go with St. Andrews in 1970. Jacklin firing eight under through the first ten holes in the first round. Lee Trevino leading after 36 and 54, and saying to Prime Minister Edward Heath on the first tee, "You ever shake hands with a Mexican?" Then the Jack Nicklaus–Doug Sanders battle in the last round and playoff, and Jack dramatically discarding one of his two sweaters to drive the last green for a birdie to narrowly win, 72–73. This after Sanders had blown a two-and-a-half-foot putt on the 72nd green that would have given him the title.

Gerald Micklem, a pillar of British golf, four-time Walker Cupper, a gent who seemed to have stepped out of a P. G. Wodehouse short story, was standing with Barbara Nicklaus in the gallery at 18 at that moment as Sanders hunched over the putt. "Congratulations," Micklem said to Barbara. "Your husband has just tied for the Open Championship." Barbara looked surprised, if not confused. Micklem added, "It looks like it breaks left, but of course it breaks right." Local knowledge. Doug didn't even hit the cup.

Favorite Quote

David Huish, the club pro at North Berwick, led through 36 holes at Carnoustie in 1975 with rounds of 69-67, but he fell apart and finished tied for thirty-second place. Not disappointed, Huish said: "I'm happy to be goin' back to Berwick and watchin' them caramel-chewers lobbin' their Dunlops into the bay."

PGA MEMORIES

SOMETIMES I WISH I'd been able to cover the PGA Championship in the quaint days of match play, which ended in 1957. It would have been fun to try to make sense of lurkers like Frank Walsh, Henry Williams, and Felice Torza making it to the finals, or trying to comprehend lurkers like Tom Creavy and Bob Hamilton actually winning it in the finals over Denny Shute and Byron Nelson. Did I say fun? I meant inconvenient.

But I've managed to make it to a total of fifty-three PGAs contested at stroke play, and that's more than enough to stock a man with a collection of agonies and ecstasies.

Assessing the Evidence

Auburn University conducted its own in-house investigation and found no evidence of any wrongdoing with Jason Dufner winning the 2013 PGA at Oak Hill.

If Only Twitter and Instagram Had Been Around Then
During Larry Nelson's winning of the 1987 PGA, his third major, at the PGA National in West Palm Beach, Florida, he was upstaged by a killer blond in a lime-green bikini who commandeered a boat to get to the floating scoreboard at the 18th hole.

Only Roman Numeral to Win a Major So Far
Davis Love III, 1997 PGA at Winged Foot

Hard to Fool a Wife
When Jack Nicklaus shot a 79 in the first round of the 1978 PGA at Oakmont, Barbara said, "He even walked sloppy."

Deep Trivia
Name the only four players who won the NCAA and the PGA. Answer: Jack Nicklaus (Ohio State), John Mahaffey (Houston), Tiger Woods (Stanford), Phil Mickelson (Arizona State).

Giving Up Smoking Could Be Hazardous to Your Golf Game
While trying to quit smoking, Arnold Palmer shot an 82 in the 1969 PGA on the NCR course in Dayton, which moved Dave Marr to tell him, "Arnold, you gave up smoking and golf the same week."

Nine Is a Crowd
That PGA in Dayton was the one where nine guys tied for the first-round lead with 69s. They were the eventual win-

ner, Raymond Floyd, and Charles Coody, Larry Ziegler, Tom Shaw, Bunky Henry, Larry Mowry, Johnny Pott, Bob Lunn, Al Geiberger. World record, far as I know.

How to WD
It was drizzling during the second round at Tanglewood in 1974 when Tom Weiskopf arrived at the 16th green. By one count, Weiskopf managed to nine-putt, occasionally gripping the putter upside down. "I'm injured and I quit," Tom announced to an official. When the official asked what his injury was, Tom said, "I'm 25 over."

It's a Whole New World
In 1996 at Valhalla, caddies rebelled and wore shorts for the first time, to combat the insufferable Louisville heat. They were told to wear pants or leave. Now it's shorts everywhere. Caddies, sportswriters—everywhere but on me.

The Shirt from Hell
It was the blue-and-white polka dot that Steve Elkington wore at Baltusrol in 2005. I take back what I wrote. It didn't look as much like a frock that Joan Crawford sold on eBay as it did Ron Turcotte's silks when he was up on Secretariat.

Fame Is Fleeting
Ed Dougherty was asked at Firestone in 1975 when he came in only two off the lead after a first-round 69 if he had ever been on a leaderboard before. He said, "Yeah, at Westchester I made four birdies in a row. But then I started going bad,

so while one guy was putting up the Y, another guy was taking down the D."

Criticisms That Make a Writer's Day

Lee Trevino at Oakmont in 1978: "The only way to stop a ball around here is call a policeman."

Jack Nicklaus in 1982 at hot, humid Southern Hills, one of the few courses where he never won a major: "I'm not sure I could play well at Southern Hills if it was air-conditioned."

Paul Goydos reviewing the renovation of Oakland Hills for the 2008 PGA: "If you had Rees Jones redo Scrabble, he would leave out all the vowels."

Tom Weiskopf commenting on George and Tom Fazio renovating Oak Hill before the 1980 PGA: "I'm going to organize a Classic Golf Course Preservation Society. Members get to carry loaded guns in case they see anybody touching a Donald Ross course."

Explanation for a Quad

André Romero explaining a 78 at Oakland Hills in 2008 that featured a quadruple 8 at number 16: "I was disconcentrated the rest of the round."

The Non-Charge

Vijay Singh won a three-hole playoff over Justin Leonard and Chris DiMarco in 2004 at Whistling Straits after a final-round 76, which was the highest last round for a winner in any major since Reg Whitcombe won the British

Open in 1938 at Sandwich with a 78 in a storm that blew down the exhibition tent.

Low Perm
Fuzzy Zoeller showed off a new hairdo while finishing second to Larry Nelson at Atlantic Athletic Club in 1981. In the locker room, Jerry Pate said to Fuzzy, "I've only seen hair like that on the back of a dog." Fuzzy's comeback: "Oh, yeah. How about you? Ever seen a bald-headed dog?"

He Used to Be a Bank Teller?
Woody Austin, after Tiger Woods's second-round 63 at Southern Hills in 2007: "I outplayed him all day, but he beat me by seven strokes . . . I don't get it."

Best Putting Exhibition
Has to be forty-five-year-old Jerry Barber at Olympia Fields in 1961. He holed three monsters on the last three holes of regulation—20 feet for birdie, 40 feet for par, and 60 feet for birdie—to tie Don January, who had been rehearsing his victory speech. Barber did it again to win the playoff, 67 to 68.

Somewhere along the way that week I was in the locker room chatting with January and a few other pros sitting around. Cary Middlecoff, Doug Sanders, Doug Ford, others. I asked what any of them thought about the phenomenal amateur Jack Nicklaus. I think it was Middlecoff who said, "If he thinks he can play, let him come out here."

Well, he did. And . . .

Best Runaway
When Rory McIlroy, the boy king, won the 2012 PGA at Kiawah by eight strokes over David Lynn with a last-round 66, it topped Jack Nicklaus winning by seven over Andy Bean at Oak Hill in 1980. Biggest runaway in a match play final belongs to Paul Runyan. He gave Sam Snead a lesson in chipping and putting at Shawnee-on-Delaware in 1938, beating him 8 and 7.

Speaking of Runaways
Jimmy Demaret used to dine out on his 10-and-9 loss to Ben Hogan in the semifinals of the 1946 PGA at Portland Golf Club. Jimmy loved for people to ask him what Hogan said during the match.

Jimmy would report, "Most of the time he'd say, 'You're away.'"

Riviera's Prank
During the '95 PGA at Riviera, a rumor floated that O. J. Simpson's handicap at the club had been mysteriously lowered in the past year of his incarceration. Pranksters apparently had been punching in low scores for him on the golf shop computer. He was now a four instead of a 16. Surely that was punishment enough.

"Save Yourself"
Gary Player was accidentally pushed into a lake in a rush of autograph seekers at Congressional in 1976. "Why didn't you jump in and save me?" Gary asked his caddie, Rabbit Dyer. Rabbit replied, "I can't swim."

Best Late Bloomer
Paul Azinger, after winning at Inverness in 1993: "Twelve years ago I'd never broken 70, and I couldn't break 80 two days in a row."

Best or Worst Prediction
John Daly after winning in '91 at Crooked Stick: "I'm not gonna become a jerk. If I become a jerk, I'll quit golf."

The Always Quotable Mr. Daly
John Daly on the subject of sports psychologists during the 2007 PGA at Southern Hills: "You gotta be insane to listen to all our s—t."

Best Rant
Tommy Bolt gets the award for his performance in the 1961 PGA at Olympia Fields near Chicago after he was suspended indefinitely—it lasted two weeks—for using "vulgar and abusive language." Part of the rant: "Man, everybody cusses. I cuss, sure, but I cuss myself, don't you see? If they suspend everybody out here who cusses, they ain't gonna have nobody left on the tour but the folks who do the suspendin'."

Don't Touch These Greens
By tournament time in '87 at the PGA National in West Palm Beach, Florida, the greens were 80 percent dirt, 10 percent wire, and 10 percent herpes.

Sudden Drama

The 1977 PGA at Pebble Beach served up the first sudden-death playoff in majors history. It was sad to see forty-seven-year-old Gene Littler stumble to a closing 76 and allow Lanny Wadkins to tie him. But in the locker room before the playoff, Lanny took the cocktail out of my hand, saying, "Gimme some of that," took a swig, said, "That ought to do it," and went out to win on the third hole.

The record book doesn't show it, but I claimed an assist.

Big Finish

The last day of the 2014 PGA at Valhalla was filled with so much drama, I've ordered a drone to drop Oscars on Rory McIlroy, Phil Mickelson, and Rickie Fowler, plus the grounds crew, which somehow managed to turn rivers and fishing holes left by a violent midday rainstorm into a golf course. Then Rory, the three-day leader and master of all golf shots, lost the lead and had to reclaim it on the last nine with an eagle and two birdies, and win it over the heroic Mickelson and the gritty Fowler with two putts practically in the dark. Best PGA ever, and one of the best majors ever. In the end, golf introduced a new sheriff in town, a twenty-five-year-old power-hitting, sweet-swinging Northern Irishman whose name wasn't Tiger.

THINNING THE HERD

THINK ABOUT A golfer whipping it around 27 holes in light-running scores of 54, 58, 55, and doing it in one day with a set of clubs that look like upside-down walking canes and a golf ball made out of congealed haggis.

Right. I'm not all that impressed with the majors that Old Tom Morris won at Prestwick on the west coast of Scotland back in the 1860s. This is not to put down majors. Majors are the gold standard by which all golfers are to be measured in this one life to live. To paraphrase an old football coach, winning majors isn't everything, it's the *only* thing.

So that's why I'm here today. To put historical evidence in the blender and identify golf's true heroes, those who reigned supreme when golf clubs looked like golf clubs and the golf ball stayed in the air longer than a shot put.

I'm permitted to do this because I know more about golf

and golf history than I do about the swords and spears of the Romans and Carthaginians.

First you have to go with me and acknowledge there were majors before there were majors. Today's majors, as ordained by Arnold Palmer, Jack Nicklaus, and the press, are the U.S. Open, British Open, and PGA, all national championships, plus the Masters, which isn't the championship of anything but became a major in the thirties due to having Bobby Jones, Grantland Rice, and a beautiful golf course going for it.

In the past there were three kinds of majors. There were the national championships. There were the old "bonus tournaments"—Western Open, North and South Open, Metropolitan Open—that awarded the winner with matching prize money from the equipment and apparel companies. There were also the events during World War Two at Chicago's Tam O'Shanter Country Club that took the place of the majors that were "suspended for the duration." Tam's events were so popular they continued through 1957. Tam's World Championship and All American Open offered obscene prize money, from first place worth $10,000 in 1951 in the World to $50,000 by 1954, along with exhibition guarantees that made winning it worth a hundred grand.

Money meant a good deal more to the touring pro back then than it does now. You couldn't tell a guy who won Tam's All American Open or World Championship that it wasn't more fun to be rich than having his name in a record book nobody reads.

But let me get on to culling golf's elite from the proletariat.

Golf's true heroes—monarchs, emperors, rulers—begin with the Great Triumvirate, and I don't mean cheeseburger, fries, and a Coke. The Great Triumvirate consisted of Harry Vardon, J. H. Taylor, and James Braid, two Englishmen and a Scot.

Vardon, Taylor, and Braid may have played golf in coats and ties, and their fans may have caught an occasional whiff of Fox and Hound pipe tobacco, but these three gentlemen dominated their competition from 1894 through 1914.

After championship golf was extended to 72 holes in 1892, which is the intelligent place to begin counting, Vardon won six British Opens and a U.S. Open while Taylor and Braid each won five British Opens. There was also a tournament called the *News of the World* Match Play Championship, which for a decade in their day was considered a major. Braid won it four times, Taylor twice, Vardon once. This gives Braid one more major than Vardon, nine to eight, an obscure stat I just kicked out of the heather.

But Vardon commands the most respect for venturing to America to win the U.S. Open of 1900 at Chicago Golf, and later tying for second in two others, the 1913 "Ouimet Open" at The Country Club in Brookline and the 1920 Open at Inverness in Toledo.

Also for inventing The Grip.

The twenties became known as "The Golden Age of Sports" primarily due to Grantland Rice and other poets flipping adjectives like pancakes while covering Babe Ruth, Ty Cobb, Jack Dempsey, Red Grange, Charley Paddock, Bill Tilden, Man o' War, and of course Bobby Jones and Walter Hagen.

Unless you've been texting and listening to rap since birth, you know that Bobby Jones won thirteen majors—all national championships—but you may not know that Walter Hagen could boast of winning seventeen over the same period.

Hagen's total would include not only his five PGAs, one of his two U.S. Opens, and four British Opens, but three of his five Western Opens, two of his three North and South Opens, and two of his three Metropolitan Opens.

Jones was movie-star handsome and did that Grand Slam thing in 1930 and grabbed the larger headlines, but it was the two of them together who lifted tournament golf into a big-time sport in the United States.

The first half of the thirties goes to Gene Sarazen. The rest of it belongs to Ralph Guldahl.

Sarazen exploded on the scene as a twenty-year-old in 1922 when he won both the U.S. Open and PGA, a historic double. He repeated in the '23 PGA, then spent the rest of the decade chasing Jones and Hagen. It was after Jones retired and Hagen was in his declining years that Sarazen inherited the earth. Sarazen won the U.S. Open and British

Open in 1932, another double. He followed this up by winning the PGA in '33 and the Masters in '35. It was his double eagle on the 15th hole at the Augusta National that got him a tie with Craig Wood in the final round, after which he won the playoff. That shot did much to major the Masters, a competition originally known as the Augusta National Invitational.

Guldahl was a slow-playing Texan from Dallas, the same age as Ben Hogan and Byron Nelson, who was considered the best player in the world from 1936 through 1939. In that stretch he won three Western Opens in a row from '36 through '38, two U.S. Opens in a row in '37 and '38, and the '39 Masters.

All that was a hallucination to Ben Hogan. At the time Ben was still struggling to make a living on the Tour. He once confided to me late in his career, "I didn't think Ralph could play a lick. He had this fast, floppy swing. I'd have been ashamed to take that swing out of town. But what he accomplished certainly made me work harder to succeed."

It was a good thing Guldahl didn't look back during his streak. He'd have noticed Byron Nelson chipping at his FootJoys.

Byron reached stardom much faster than Hogan, like five years faster. Nelson was stronger and taller than Ben, a natural athlete, unlike Ben, and almost chose professional baseball over golf. Byron won the Metropolitan Open in '36, the Masters in '37. In '39 he won the U.S. Open, the Western Open, and the North and South Open, and would have accomplished a sort of American Slam had he not lost to Henry Picard in the PGA final on the 37th hole.

Nelson owned most of the forties. He won the '40 PGA, the '42 Masters, the '45 PGA, and the All American Opens at Tam in '44 and '45. It was in '45, of course, that he did the streak thing. Along the way he was runner-up in the '41 Masters, PGA, and Western Open, the '44 PGA, and the '46 U.S. Open.

After announcing that he was retiring at the start of the '46 season, he went on to win six more tournaments, two of which were in Houston and New Orleans, where Ben Hogan and Sam Snead finished second and third.

Byron acted as if it was "a strange thing" rather than something to be proud of that he held an edge over Hogan and Snead in head-to-head duels.

He topped Hogan in close contests in a playoff for the '40 Texas Open, in a quarterfinal match of the '41 PGA, and in their exciting playoff for the '42 Masters. He dusted Snead in the PGA final of '40, in a 36-hole playoff for the Charlotte Open in '45, and in that two-day 72-hole exhibition match in '45 that was billed as a "World Championship of Golf."

"It was a funny thing," Byron liked to say. "Ben and Sam were two of the greatest players in the world, but they never could beat me head-to-head. I don't know why that was. It was just the funniest thing."

———

Ben Hogan and Sam Snead dominated golf from the latter half of '46 through 1956. The press saw them as bitter rivals. They were rivals on the golf course, to be sure, but it was known to a few of us that they were close friends. Ben was in awe of Sam's picture swing and entertained by Sam's locker room humor. Sam was in awe of Ben's fierce work ethic and competitive spirit.

They intruded on Byron Nelson's dynasty, and for a time the three of them were considered another Great Triumvirate. What brought this about was Hogan winning the North-South in '40 and '42, winning the '42 U.S. "wartime" Open at Ridgemoor in Chicago—it would become known as Ben's fifth U.S. Open, although "unofficial"— being runner-up to Nelson in that '42 Masters, and in '46 winning the PGA, Western Open, and a third North-South. Meanwhile, Sam was winning the '42 PGA and the '46 British Open, and finishing runner-up in eight other majors.

I enjoy pointing out that Hogan specialized in Triple Crowns. You know about '53, when he won the Masters, U.S. Open, and British Open. But you may not know about the others: In '46 he won the PGA, Western Open, and North-South Open. In '48 he won the U.S. Open, PGA, and Western Open. In '51 he captured the U.S. Open, Masters, and World Championship at Tam O'Shanter.

Snead took advantage of Hogan's absence in '49 when Ben's Cadillac lost a bout to the Greyhound bus. Sam practically ran the table. He won the Masters, PGA, Western Open, and North-South Open, and narrowly lost the U.S. Open by three-putting the 71st green at Medinah. That would have been a Big Five, or a Cinco de Sneado. Maybe something more poetic.

I give Hogan sixteen majors and eight runner-ups. I give Snead twelve majors and a whopping thirteen runner-ups. And the two of them did it against an array of combatants that included Lloyd Mangrum, Cary Middlecoff, Jimmy Demaret, Jackie Burke, Tommy Bolt, Julius Boros, Bobby Locke, and more Dutch Harrisons, Johnny Bullas, and Chick Harberts than you can count.

There's been one more Great Triumvirate in golf, and if you don't know it consisted of Jack Nicklaus, Arnold Palmer, and Gary Player, I will confiscate your press badge and sentence you to cover NASCAR.

What can be said about Nicklaus, Palmer, and Player that you don't already know? That Jack's middle name is William? That Arnold's middle name is Daniel? That Gary doesn't have a middle name?

It's accepted that these three won a total of thirty-four majors between them from 1958 through 1986. Breaking them down, Nicklaus has eighteen, Player nine, Palmer seven. You could win money betting that Player has more majors than Palmer. The average guy doesn't buy it. The average guy will say, "How can this be? Arnold Palmer invented golf on TV. Arnold Palmer took golf to the people. Arnold Palmer is more loved than Lassie."

One explanation is that Arnold lost a lot of majors he could have won or should have won if it hadn't been for a fellow named Destiny, who is known to be as untrustworthy as an airline pilot with a thirst.

As for the number thirty-four for the Big Three, I'm upping it to forty. First, I'm removing the quote marks from "the fifth major." The Players in Ponte Vedra Beach offers the biggest paycheck on the Tour for the winner, and annually attracts the strongest field. Guys would trade a lot of Greensboros for one Players trophy.

Nicklaus won the Players three out of the first five years of its existence, so I give him three more majors. Then I'm invoking the Bobby Jones Rule. This rule says if a guy wins a pro major, he gets to count his U.S. Amateur title if he has one. Jack has two and Arnold has one. New count: Nicklaus has twenty-three majors; Palmer has eight.

Don't scream. I'll be applying the same arithmetic to Tiger Woods and Phil Mickelson before this exercise is over.

Despite the dominance of Jack, Arnold, and Gary over those twenty-nine years, there was an interlude of fourteen seasons—'68 through '84—when they had to contend with two brash upstarts named Tom Watson and Lee Trevino.

Watson won eight majors—five British Opens, two Masters, and one U.S. Open. In doing so he turned Nicklaus into a runner-up four times, a feat that once prompted Jack to tell him, "You little s.o.b., you're something else."

Trevino won seven majors—two U.S. Opens, two British Opens, two PGAs, and one Players. He also turned Nicklaus into a runner-up in four majors. The most stunning was in the '72 British Open at Muirfield, when Jack was going for the pro slam, having won the Masters and U.S. Open.

After his victory, Lee said, in typical fashion, "I didn't come over here to try to help Jack Nicklaus win the Grand Slam."

The period from 1986 through 1996 was dreary for America. True, Nicklaus won a sixth Masters, Ben Crenshaw won a second Masters, and Curtis Strange won back-to-back U.S. Opens, but foreigners kidnapped most of the majors. When the dust settled, England's Nick Faldo and Australia's Greg Norman had made the biggest impressions.

Faldo won three Masters and three British Opens, while Norman was a constant presence. Greg seemed forever to be threatening, and he did win two British Opens and a Players. His career featured eight runner-ups and a total of eighteen finishes in the top five. Some of his meltdowns were self-imposed, but he had the misfortune of losing twice to miracle hole-outs—the bunker shot by Bob Tway on the last hole in the '86 PGA and the long pitch by Larry Mize in sudden death at the '87 Masters.

Meanwhile, it was a decade in which One-Hit Wonders ruined golf stories. There were eleven of them. Among the batch: Jeff Sluman, Wayne Grady, Ian Baker-Finch, Steve Jones, Mark Brooks—dare I go on?

If Jack Nicklaus has twenty-three majors, Tiger Woods now has nineteen currently. Together with his four Masters, four

PGAs, three U.S. Opens, and three British Opens, I'm adding Tiger's three U.S. Amateurs—the Bobby Jones Rule—and his two wins in the Players.

In this reign of Tiger as a rock star, which seems like a hundred years, only two competitors have stepped up to own part of the turf—Phil Mickelson and Rory McIlroy. Phil's accumulation of majors rises to seven when his U.S. Amateur of 1990 and his Players win in 2007 are added to his three Masters, one PGA, and the 2013 British Open, where he shot that mind-blowing, come-from-behind final-round 66. Meanwhile, Rory has captured one U.S. Open, one British Open, and two PGAs by the age of twenty-five.

There hasn't been a golf swing as sound and yet picturesque as McIlroy's since, well, I guess Sam Snead. The boy king has it all, plus he's incredibly likable. He alone makes the future of pro golf exciting.

The most curious stat in Phil's career is that he's been a runner-up in a record six U.S. Opens. Six. You would think that sheer luck would have let him win one or two of those.

Luck, of course, plays by its own rules. Otherwise, how could Jack Fleck have ever beaten Ben Hogan in a U.S. Open playoff?

Scooping up the old recognized majors and throwing them in a pile with today's recognized majors, here, as of this writing, is my new count of the all-time multiple winners of golf's major championships:

Jack Nicklaus—23 (6 Masters, 5 PGAs, 4 U.S. Opens, 3 British Opens, 3 Players, 2 U.S. Amateurs)

Walter Hagen—22 (5 PGAs, 5 Western Opens, 4 British Opens, 2 U.S. Opens, 3 North-South Opens, 3 Metropolitan Opens)

Tiger Woods—19 (4 Masters, 4 PGAs, 3 U.S. Opens, 3 British Opens, 2 Players, 3 U.S. Amateurs)

Ben Hogan—16 (5 U.S. Opens, 2 Masters, 2 PGAs, 1 British Open, 2 Western Opens, 3 North-South Opens, 1 Tam O'Shanter World Championship)

Bobby Jones—13 (4 U.S. Opens, 3 British Opens, 5 U.S. Amateurs, 1 British Amateur)

Sam Snead—12 (3 Masters, 3 PGAs, 1 British Open, 3 North-South Opens, 2 Western Opens)

Byron Nelson—10 (2 Masters, 2 PGAs, 1 U.S. Open, 1 Western Open, 1 North-South Open, 1 Metropolitan Open, 2 Tam O'Shanter All American Opens)

Gene Sarazen—9 (2 U.S. Opens, 3 PGAs, 1 Masters, 1 British Open, 1 Western Open, 1 Metropolitan Open)

Gary Player—9 (3 Masters, 3 British Opens, 2 PGAs, 1 U.S. Open)

"Long Jim" Barnes—9 (2 PGAs, 1 U.S. Open, 1 British Open, 3 Western Opens, 2 North-South Opens)

James Braid—9 (5 British Opens, 4 *News of the World* Match Plays)

Arnold Palmer—8 (4 Masters, 2 British Opens, 1 U.S. Open, 1 U.S. Amateur)

Tom Watson—8 (5 British Opens, 2 Masters, 1 U.S. Open)

Harry Vardon—8 (6 British Opens, 1 U.S. Open, 1 *News of the World* Match Play)

Willie Anderson—8 (4 U.S. Opens, 4 Western Opens)

Alex Smith—8 (2 U.S. Opens, 2 Western Opens, 4 Metropolitan Opens)

Lee Trevino—7 (2 U.S. Opens, 2 British Opens, 2 PGAs, 1 Players)

Phil Mickelson—7 (3 Masters, 1 British Open, 1 PGA, 1 Players, 1 U.S. Amateur)

Macdonald Smith—7 (3 Western Opens, 3 Metropolitan Opens, 1 North-South Open)

J. H. Taylor—7 (5 British Opens, 2 *News of the World* Match Plays)

Harold Hilton—7 (2 British Opens, 4 British Amateurs, 1 U.S. Amateur)

Alec Ross—7 (1 U.S. Open, 6 North-South Opens)

Nick Faldo—6 (3 Masters, 3 British Opens)

Ralph Guldahl—6 (2 U.S. Opens, 3 Western Opens, 1 Masters)

Henry Picard—6 (1 Masters, 1 PGA, 2 North-South Opens, 2 Metropolitan Opens)

Jock Hutchison—6 (1 British Open, 1 PGA, 1 U.S. "wartime" Open, 2 Western Opens, 1 North-South Open)

Bobby Locke—6 (5 British Opens, 1 Tam O'Shanter All American Open)

Seve Ballesteros—5 (3 British Opens, 2 Masters)

Raymond Floyd—5 (2 PGAs, 1 U.S. Open, 1 Masters, 1 Players)

Julius Boros—5 (2 U.S. Opens, 1 PGA, 2 Tam O'Shanter World Championships)

Lloyd Mangrum—5 (1 U.S. Open, 2 Western Opens, 1 Tam O'Shanter All American Open, 1 Tam O'Shanter World Championship)

Cary Middlecoff—5 (2 U.S. Opens, 1 Masters, 1 Western Open, 1 North-South Open)

Tommy Armour—5 (1 U.S. Open, 1 British Open, 1 PGA, 1 Western Open, 1 Metropolitan Open)

Lawson Little—5 (1 U.S. Open, 2 U.S. Amateurs, 2 British Amateurs)

Paul Runyan—5 (2 PGAs, 2 North-South Opens, 1 Metropolitan Open)

Jerry Travers—5 (1 U.S. Open, 4 U.S. Amateurs)

Peter Thomson—5 (5 British Opens)

Rory McIlroy—4 (1 U.S. Open, 1 British Open, 2 PGAs)

Ernie Els—4 (2 U.S. Opens, 2 British Opens)

Nick Price—4 (2 PGAs, 1 British Open, 1 Players)

Jimmy Demaret—4 (3 Masters, 1 Western Open)

Horton Smith—4 (2 Masters, 2 North-South Opens)

Chick Evans—4 (1 U.S. Open, 1 Western Open, 2 U.S. Amateurs)

Hal Sutton—4 (1 PGA, 2 Players, 1 U.S. Amateur)

Tom McNamara—4 (2 North-South Opens, 1 Western Open, 1 Metropolitan Open)

Gil Nicholls—4 (2 North-South Opens, 2 Metropolitan Opens)

Francis Ouimet—3 (1 U.S. Open, 2 U.S. Amateurs)

John J. McDermott—3 (2 U.S. Opens, 1 Western Open)

Willie Macfarlane—3 (1 U.S. Open, 2 Metropolitan Opens)

Fred McLeod—3 (1 U.S. Open, 2 North-South Opens)

Olin Dutra—3 (1 U.S. Open, 1 PGA, 1 Metropolitan Open)

Denny Shute—3 (2 PGAs, 1 British Open)

Craig Wood—3 (1 U.S. Open, 1 Masters, 1 Metropolitan Open)

José María Olazábal—3 (2 Masters, 1 British Amateur)

Henry Cotton—3 (3 British Opens)

Mike Brady—3 (1 North-South Open, 1 Western Open, 1 Metropolitan Open)

Johnny Palmer—3 (1 PGA, 1 Western Open, 1 Tam O'Shanter World Championship)

Payne Stewart—3 (2 U.S. Opens, 1 PGA)

Greg Norman—3 (2 British Opens, 1 Players)

Billy Casper—3 (2 U.S. Opens, 1 Masters)

Hale Irwin—3 (3 U.S. Opens)

Mark O'Meara—3 (1 Masters, 1 British Open, 1 U.S. Amateur)

Lanny Wadkins—3 (1 PGA, 1 Players, 1 U.S. Amateur)

Jerry Pate—3 (1 U.S. Open, 1 Players, 1 U.S. Amateur)

Vijay Singh—3 (2 PGAs, 1 Masters)

Larry Nelson—3 (1 U.S. Open, 2 PGAs)

Fred Couples—3 (1 Masters, 2 Players)

Davis Love III—3 (1 PGA, 2 Players)

Sandy Lyle—3 (1 British Open, 1 Masters, 1 Players)

Lee Janzen—3 (2 U.S. Opens, 1 Players)

Steve Elkington—3 (1 PGA, 2 Players)

Justin Leonard—3 (1 British Open, 1 Players, 1 U.S. Amateur)

Padraig Harrington—3 (2 British Opens, 1 PGA)

Martin Kaymer—3 (1 U.S. Open, 1 PGA, 1 Players)

Johnny Miller—2 (1 U.S. Open, 1 British Open)

Ben Crenshaw—2 (2 Masters)

Curtis Strange—2 (2 U.S. Opens)

Jackie Burke—2 (1 Masters, 1 PGA)

Gene Littler—2 (1 U.S. Open, 1 U.S. Amateur)

Tommy Bolt—2 (1 U.S. Open, 1 North-South Open)

Fuzzy Zoeller—2 (1 U.S. Open, 1 Masters)

Tony Jacklin—2 (1 U.S. Open, 1 British Open)

Hubert Green—2 (1 U.S. Open, 1 PGA)

David Graham—2 (1 U.S. Open, 1 PGA)

Tom Kite—2 (1 U.S. Open, 1 Players)

John Daly—2 (1 PGA, 1 British Open)

Dave Stockton—2 (2 PGAs)

Andy North—2 (2 U.S. Opens)

Doug Ford—2 (1 Masters, 1 PGA)

Johnny Revolta—2 (1 PGA, 1 Western Open)

Leo Diegel—2 (2 PGAs)

Bobby Cruickshank—2 (2 North-South Opens)

Jimmy Hines—2 (2 Metropolitan Opens)

Johnny Farrell—2 (1 U.S. Open, 1 Metropolitan Open)

Ted Ray—2 (1 U.S. Open, 1 British Open)

Vic Ghezzi—2 (1 PGA, 1 North-South Open)

Lew Worsham—2 (1 U.S. Open, 1 Tam O'Shanter World Championship)

Dick Mayer—2 (1 U.S. Open, 1 Tam O'Shanter World Championship)

Billy Burke—2 (1 U.S. Open, 1 North-South Open)

Jimmy Turnesa—2 (1 PGA, 1 North-South Open)

Johnny Goodman—2 (1 U.S. Open, 1 U.S. Amateur)

"Wild Bill" Melhorn—2 (1 Western Open, 1 Metropolitan Open)

Laurie Aucterlonie—2 (1 U.S. Open, 1 Western Open)

Robert Simpson—2 (2 Western Opens)

Bob Hamilton—2 (1 PGA, 1 North-South Open)

Bob MacDonald—2 (2 Metropolitan Opens)

Craig Stadler—2 (1 Masters, 1 U.S. Amateur)

Al Geiberger—2 (1 PGA, 1 Players)

John Mahaffey—2 (1 PGA, 1 Players)

David Duval—2 (1 British Open, 1 Players)

Retief Goosen—2 (2 U.S. Opens)

Angel Cabrera—2 (1 U.S. Open, 1 Masters)

Bubba Watson—2 (2 Masters)

Adam Scott—2 (1 Masters, 1 Players)

Matt Kuchar—2 (1 Players, 1 U.S. Amateur)

Sergio Garcia—2 (1 Players, 1 British Amateur)

Jordan Spieth—2 (1 Masters, 1 U.S. Open)

Zack Johnson—2 (1 Masters, 1 British Open)

Names make news. Works for me.

LITERATURE MEETS GOLF, OR
TRUE FICTION RIDES AGAIN

I F I'D HAD to entertain another "celebrity author" at the Masters like the one last year, I might have given up golf and reading altogether. In the first place, I wasn't impressed that Barrett Saunders had won the National Book Award for his novel *Gavin Seems Bored*. And I wasn't overwhelmed that his work was said to break new literary ground when he proved that an entire novel could be written in one paragraph.

I would never know.

But I do know that the struggle to educate Barrett Saunders about the game of golf, the Augusta National Golf Club, and the Masters tournament itself was beyond tiresome.

Yes, those flowers are real. Yes, those trees are very old. Yes, "a good many women" have always attended. No, the men in green jackets are not part of an orchestra. Who is that man carrying the other man's "luggage"? He's called a caddie.

I should explain that I've been doing this since Ben Hogan's day. The magazine I work for invites a well-known person from the literary world to attend the Masters every year. The person stays with us, we writers and editors, in the well-appointed private home we rent during Masters Week every spring. What we ask of our special guest is that he or she cast a "fresh eye" on the Masters scene and write an article for next year's preview issue.

I knew there'd be trouble with Barrett Saunders when I took him to the course for his first look around on Wednesday. As he stood on the clubhouse veranda and gazed about, he said, "Well, I can tell you this much. Your rather baroque sport seems to require an inordinate amount of space."

The magazine never ran the story that Barrett Saunders submitted. I heard from the editors that it was excruciatingly long, experimented with punctuation, and "challenged" their sanity.

Over the years we've had various experiences at the tournament with high-profile authors. These stand out in my memory:

Marlowe Investigates

In 1953 we made the mistake of inviting Raymond Chandler, having been unaware that he hated golf and rich people. This was the year Ben Hogan set the Masters record and went on to capture the Triple Crown. Chandler ignored Ben Hogan's performance and sent us a one-graf piece, which read:

Marlowe knew he was calling on five million dollars, but

money never impressed him. Money couldn't dodge a bullet or play the ukulele. He drove through the row of magnolias and parked at the entrance to the white mansion. He marched through the clubhouse and out onto the veranda and found the cabin where the man lived and conducted his business. Marlowe barged through the cabin door, pulled up a chair, torched a Chesterfield, propped his feet up on the dictator's gilt-edged desk, and told Chairman Clifford Roberts exactly what he thought of his Banana Republic.

A Farewell to Hemingway

We were ecstatic in 1961 when Ernest Hemingway accepted our invitation. Just in time, I might add. He was only three months away from going to Idaho and scoring a hole in one on his head with a shotgun.

This was the April when everyone got so mad that Arnold Palmer double-bogeyed the last hole to give Gary Player the Masters. Hemingway had studied the 18th hole from a distance and said it reminded him of Kilimanjaro, except there were golfers on it instead of a leopard.

Hemingway said, "Palmer was good and true and strong. He did not win, but isn't it pretty to think so?"

He grew angrier the more he thought about the result.

"I want to blow a bridge," he said.

"Which one?" I said. "The Sarazen, the Hogan, or the Nelson?"

"I will let Anselmo choose. It will be good and true and strong. We will blow the bridge and I will come back to Maria."

"What if you don't come back?" I said.

He said, "A man can be destroyed but he can't be defeated. If I don't come back, Maria and I will always have what we had. Mostly short sentences."

The Jolter and Marilyn

A year later, in 1962, we managed to lure Joltin' Joe DiMaggio and Marilyn Monroe to the Masters. They had remained close friends after their famous nine-month marriage in 1954 had crumbled in divorce.

Joe, we were told, took up golf after he retired from the Yankees.

Two of our staff writers questioned how Joe and Marilyn qualified as "literary figures." No problem, our editors said. Surely over the past eight years they had read three or four books between them.

Joe never went to the golf course. He stayed in our rental house and remained silent and sullen the entire week. When he wasn't chipping in the yard he sat alone at the dining room table telling the housekeepers that when baseball stopped being fun, it was no longer a game. Marilyn went to the course every day but learned to dress differently after Friday. The breeze across the veranda kept blowing her white skirt up to her waist. Caused a bit of a commotion.

This was the year Arnold Palmer defeated Gary Player and Dow Finsterwald in an 18-hole playoff. Marilyn followed the drama.

When she came home that evening she found us lounging in the living room.

She rushed up to DiMaggio and said, "Joe, you've never heard such cheering!"

DiMaggio quietly said, "Yes, I have."

Gay Talese, a young writer for the *New York Times*, had been invited to our house that night. He overheard the exchange. Said he could use it someday in a magazine piece.

Dottie's Poem

Dorothy Parker was my favorite guest. The year was 1966. She was in her early seventies, but there was still a hint of the beauty she once was, and her mind was as sharp as if she were still sitting around the Algonquin Round Table with Woollcott, Kaufman, and the gang.

I sat with her at a table on the veranda the one day she spent with us in Augusta. What a quick learner she was about golf. She caught on right away that Arnold Palmer, Gary Player, and Jack Nicklaus were the giants of the era.

In an admiring moment, I said to her, "Why do I think you were the wittiest person at the Algonquin Round Table?"

"Because I was, darling," she said.

She wrote a takeoff for us on her famous Byron, Shelley, and Keats poem.

> *Palmer and Player and Nicklaus*
> *Were a Big Three that never tricked us.*
> *Arnie's Army continually roared,*
> *Gary had moments adored,*
> *And Jack's victories, oh how they soared!*
> *How wonderfully often they'd lift us,*
> *This Palmer and Player,*
> *This Palmer and Player and Nicklaus.*

The Injustice of It All

The timing couldn't have been worse for John Steinbeck and his Dust Bowl friend, Tom Joad. They joined us in 1968, and that was the year Roberto De Vicenzo signed an incorrect scorecard and lost the Masters. Or at least a chance to win it in a playoff with Bob Goalby.

For those who may have forgotten the details of the incident, Roberto shot a brilliant 65 in the final round to tie Goalby at 277. But his playing companion, Tommy Aaron, who was keeping his card, somehow wrote down a par 4 instead of a birdie 3 on the 17th hole, and Roberto witlessly approved it. The error in arithmetic gave him a 66 and 278 for second place.

The Masters committeemen were sick about it, but they saw no way around the rules of golf. The rules of golf are sacred.

The likable Argentinean accepted the disappointment as best he could, saying to the press, "What a stupid I am."

The unfortunate incident didn't sit well with John Steinbeck, always a champion of the downtrodden.

"It's tragic," he said. "A man fights his way out of the tortilla flats and cannery rows to get here, and this happens to him."

"I think he grew up caddying," I said. "Anyhow, he's played here four or five times. In fact, he finished tenth last year."

Ignoring that, Steinbeck said, "It's proof again of something I've observed in life. If you're in trouble, or hurt, or in need, go to the poor people. They're the ones that'll help you."

Then Steinbeck asked if there were any poor people nearby.

I said, "We might find one or two at a public course."

When we returned to the house, having not come across any poor people, we found Tom Joad in his dirty shirt and ragged *Grapes of Wrath* cap on a rant about the injustice that had befallen Roberto De Vicenzo. He was saying he was going to fight it the rest of his life.

"I'll be aroun' in the dark," Tom Joad said. "I'll be everywhere—everywhere you look. Wherever there's a golfer gettin' beat up by a PGA rules official, I'll be there. Wherever there's a golfer bein' told he's out of bounds when he ain't, I'll be there. Wherever there's a golfer bein' told by a USGA guy he don't deserve a free drop, I'll be there. Wherever there's . . ."

Tom Joad kept righting the wrongs of the world as Steinbeck nodded and listened intently. Soon enough, however, the rest of us retreated to the kitchen and dipped into the fried chicken and baked ham.

TALKING HEADS

HEY, GREAT. THE golf is on.

"Chuck, I'm continually amazed at how many fine young men we have out here. I don't know any sport where we have so many fine young men to cover. We're lucky guys, you and me, being around all these fine young men."

"Right you are, Ted. When you're looking for a group of fine young men today, you don't need to look any further than where we are right now. Some say NASCAR, bowling, tractor pull, the military. I say the PGA Tour."

"I couldn't have put it better myself."

"Speaking of fine young men, here comes one now. Timmy Jack Kendrick. He's got a difficult chip here, Ted."

"Yes, he does, Chuck. Timmy Jack hit a wonderful second shot, like so many of them do, but it caught up in the fringe. But I expect him to handle this chip without much trouble, talented player that he is."

"We know how much he wants it, don't we, Ted? Not just for himself, but for his lovely wife, Dawn, and his two youngsters, Chip and Cracker. For his mom and dad too, of course, back home in Iowa, or maybe it's Indiana. Wherever the moonlight shines on the sycamores."

"Yes, and we should add his minister, the Reverend Dr. R. S. Hatcher. I see the reverend down there in the crowd. The Rev loves the game and follows the Tour every chance he gets. Timmy Jack seems to be studying this chip from every angle. These fine young men never leave much to chance, do they, Chuck?"

"You won't get a sour note out of me on *that* subject, Ted. These fine young men strive for perfection like no other athletes I've encountered."

"You know, Timmy Jack got a bad break on that approach shot. It should have been up there stiff to put him eight under on the last eight holes. Man, the birdies are flying. And that's on what I consider to be as tough a layout as there is. Tip's got a 58 in the crosshairs if he can get it up and down. But you can't say enough about this golf course, can you? Talk about a rugged test."

"No, you can't, Ted. And you can't say enough about the hardworking members who put so much of their time and energy into making this a blue-ribbon stop on the tour. Not to overlook what this club contributes to charitable causes."

"Nicely said, Chuck. If I may, I'd like to drop in a word about the title sponsor, RealMeat.com. This is the company's fourth year in golf, and I must say they're as excited as ever to be associated with these fine young men who've worked so hard to become a part of what I call the upper echelon of the game."

"It was terrific fun last night, wasn't it? Having dinner with Mace Lawson, the CEO of Real Meat, and his assistant, Pete Scogie. Great guys. I see Timmy Jack is ready to golf his ball, as we say out here. What do you think he'll try to do with it, Ted?"

"I wouldn't be surprised to see him chip it in. I think he'll take it up the slope, a couple of inches inside the fur, as we call it, and let it slide down to the left, then make the slow curve back to the right. I say if he gets the speed right, it cruises straight into the jaws. We know how badly he wants that 57."

"Indeed, we do. Uh-oh. That's not exactly what he had in mind, is it? He stubbed it or something. He's left himself— what—thirty feet short?"

"Somewhere in that range, Chuck. Not a pretty sound, is it? That groan from the gallery? I call it the chorus of heartbreak."

"Ted, that is *so* descriptive."

"Thank you, Chuck."

"I've got shivers."

"Thank you again, but this is not about me. It's about Timmy Jack Kendrick. He has a good excuse for the chip in my book. Those photographers down there made a lot of noise on his backswing. These press people, I'm telling you. They'll never understand that these fine young men are just out here trying to make a living for their families."

"That wasn't his middle finger, was it?"

"What middle finger?"

"The gesture Timmy Jack gave that woman."

"I didn't see it. I can't report what I didn't see."

"He gave her the old . . . you know."

"I'm sure he was saying, 'I'm still Number One out here, whether you like it or not, lady.'"

"If you say so. Whoa! He's left this one short, too, Ted. It looks like fifteen feet short, and it was downhill. Goodness me."

"It's that darn grain. These greens are absolutely perfect— I'll take 'em over my living room carpet. But they do have their uneven spots, as all the rest of us do in this thing called life. But there's no give-up in this young man. Like all the others out here. Down to the last man to miss the cut. Not an ounce of give-up."

"Wow. Timmy Jack just walked up and rammed this one ten feet by. He's not in the best frame of mind right now, is he, Ted?"

"He'll regroup. That's what these fine young men do."

"There's still some commotion going on between Timmy Jack and that woman. Do you see our foot soldier down there anywhere?"

"We don't call them 'foot soldiers' anymore, Chuck. Gotta watch the slip of the tongue. Jason is our *on-course correspondent*. 'Foot soldier' has always been demeaning in my estimation. I believe I see Jason over there behind the bunker on the left. Hey, ho, Jason. What have you got for us?"

"It's a pretty nasty situation, guys. The lady seems to have some sort of issue with Timmy Jack. She's been heckling him the last two holes."

"She looks rather attractive from up here, Jason."

"She is, as a matter of fact."

"Any idea what this is about?"

"All I can say is, they apparently know each other from somewhere."

"We'll be coming back to you, Jason."

"Oh no!"

"What, Ted?"

"Timmy Jack just missed it from a foot. He's heading for a triple, maybe a quad."

"Well, that's a darn shame. As I've said before about composure . . ."

"My God! He just pulled down his pants. He's mooning the cup . . . and the woman. Shouldn't that be considered conduct unbecom . . . ?"

"They're screaming in the truck, Ted!"

"Back in two, golf fans."

HIS OWNSELF
A Semi-Memoir

In *His Ownself*, Dan Jenkins takes us on a tour of his legendary career as a sportswriter and novelist. Here we see Dan hone his craft, from his high school paper through to his first job at the Fort Worth Press and on to the glory days of *Sports Illustrated*. Whether in Texas, New York, or anywhere for that matter, Dan was always at the center of it all—hanging out at Elaine's while swapping stories with politicians and movie stars, covering every Masters and U.S. Open and British Open for over four decades. The result is a knee-slapping, star-studded, once-in-a-lifetime memoir from one of the most important, hilarious, and semi-cantankerous sportswriters ever.

Sports/Autobiography

THE FRANCHISE BABE

Jack Brannon, a golf writer in his forties who has been bunkered more than once in the marriage game, covers the sport for a big-time magazine. Bored with the PGA, he decides to check out "the Lolitas," on the LPGA Tour. Jack chooses as a magazine subject Ginger Clayton, a fiery eighteen-year old whose killer looks and killer game make her the kind of star who can take the LPGA to the next level. She is, indeed, The Franchise Babe, and everyone wants a part of her, but someone, it seems, is trying to knock Ginger out of the competition-permanently. Filled with dead-on take downs of sports moms, adventurous promoters, suck-up corporate sponsors, double-dealing sports agents, and just enough menace to make golf dangerous, Dan Jenkins' latest tale of hijinks on the links is not to be missed.

Fiction

JENKINS AT THE MAJORS
*Sixty Years of the World's Best Golf Writing,
from Hogan to Tiger*

In this seminal collection, Dan Jenkins has selected the funniest and most riveting stories from his epic career as a writer for *Sports Illustrated* and *Golf Digest*, where his wry reportage of golf's most thrilling finishes, historic moments, and heartbreaking collapses brought legions of fans intimately close to the action. All the greatest moments of golf over the last sixty years are here: Jack Nicklaus at Pebble Beach, Arnold Palmer at Cherry Hills, Ben Hogan and Sam Snead at Oakmont, and of course Tiger Woods, just about everywhere. As much about journalism and watching the growth of one of our most cherished sports writers, as it is about the great game of golf, *Jenkins at the Majors* is a must read for sports fans and golfers alike.

Sports

ALSO AVAILABLE

Bubba Talks

Dead Solid Perfect

Fairways and Greens

*The Money-Whipped Steer-Job
Three-Jack Give-Up Artist*

Slim and None

ANCHOR BOOKS
Available wherever books are sold.
www.anchorbooks.com